THE UPPER ARKANSAS RIVER

D1595814

A river is never quite silent; it can never of its very nature, be quite still; it is never quite the same from one day to the next. It has its own life and its own beauty, and the creatures it nourishes are alive and beautiful also.

from *A River Never Sleeps*
by Roderick Haig-Brown, 1944

THE UPPER ARKANSAS RIVER

Rapids, History & Nature Mile by Mile

From Granite to the
Pueblo Reservoir

FRANK STAUB

with contributions by
Peter Anderson

FULCRUM, INC.
GOLDEN, COLORADO
1988

Book Design by Chris Bierwirth

Maps by Margaret Deluca, animal drawings by Nancy Vickery, geological diagrams by Richard Christiansen, and photographs by Frank Staub unless credited otherwise.

Library of Congress Cataloging-in-Publication Data

Staub, Frank J. The upper Arkansas, rapids, history, and nature mile by mile. Bibliography: p.
  1. White-water canoeing—Arkansas River—Guide-books.
  2. Rafting (Sports)—Arkansas River—Guide-books.
  3. Arkansas River—Description and travel—Guide-books.
I. Anderson, Peter, 1935-   II. Title.
GV776.A8S73   1987   917.67   87-27439
ISBN 1-55591-021-1 (soft)

Printed in the United States of America
1 2 3 4 5 6 7 8 9 0

FULCRUM, INC.
Golden, Colorado

PREFACE

Only a handful of people have the time and money for a multiday trip on a great American wilderness river such as the Colorado through the Grand Canyon or the Salmon's Middle Fork. So for many of us, more accessible rivers like the Arkansas have become worthy substitutes. Those who require vast tracts of undeveloped land surrounding the rivers they travel might dismiss the Arkansas as being too civilized. But the grand views and challenging rapids in the Arkansas' exquisite backcountry sections like Browns Canyon and the Royal Gorge rival those of the West's more remote waterways. This fact, along with the Arkansas' proximity to the urbanized Front Range, has made it Colorado's number one river for whitewater boating—surpassing even the state's great namesake stream in popularity.

The purposes of this book are: to promote safer and more enjoyable boating; to help satisfy the river traveler's curiosity about the Arkansas' history, geology and biology; and to encourage a desire to preserve the river's scenic and natural qualities.

It's also hoped that this book can be used as a textbook for commercial guide trainees (but not a substitute for a qualified instructor) as well as an information source for anyone interested in the Arkansas Valley even if they never travel on the river itself.

This book is dedicated to the
Arkansas river-running community.

Contents

ACKNOWLEDGMENTS

A project of this magnitude requires the input of many people. Peter Anderson's ability to turn the yarns and legends of the old West into colorful, written narratives is revealed in the history entries in chapter 4. Mark Emmer's help with computer matters was invaluable. I'm very grateful to Mike Portnoy, Hughey Hardy, Bruce Loeffler, Richard Christiansen and Ken Klco for the information they provided on the geology of the Arkansas Valley. Thanks also to Rick Anderson, Fred Rasmussen, Donald L. Puterbaugh and Vern Rutherford for their counsel in aquatic biology. Mattie Augustine provided some historical information about the Arkansas Canyon. J. Boyd, Jack Chivvis, Karen and Reid Dils, Bob Hamel, Ray Kitzen, Pete Makris, Kelly O'Connor, Stu Pappenfort, Casey Swansen and Dave Tunison all supplied comments for the river trips section. Assistance was also provided by Dave Smith, Carl and Nancy Florey, Martha and Ed Quillen, Norma Edlin, Bruce Bowerle and Paul Trentzsch. Finally, I'd like to thank Hunter Holloway, Betsy Armstrong and the rest of the staff at Fulcrum, Inc. for their wisdom in seeing the value of this project and for their efforts toward its completion.

How to Use this Book

Chapters 1 and 2 in part I provide a general look at the Arkansas while chapters 3 and 4 in part II examine the river in more detail on a mile-by-mile basis.

Chapter 1, "The River's Story," covers the Arkansas' history, geology and biology. Anyone navigating a raft, canoe or kayak down the Arkansas should read the comments about boating in chapter 2. Chapter 3 describes principal access points, major rapids, bridges, dams etc. for the most commonly run half-day and all-day trips from just above Granite to the Pueblo Reservoir. Chapter 4 contains additional information about the Arkansas Valley's human and natural history with reference to specific points along the river.

The maps in part II are marked with mile numbers referred to in the text.

This book has not been waterproofed and should be stored in a waterproof container when carried on a boat. Ziplock plastic bags are excellent for this purpose as they allow the book to be stuffed between chest and lifejacket and pulled out for quick reference between rapids.

Although this book is designed to be used as a guide during river trips, it can also be used as a reference during sightseeing tours on the roads which parallel the Arkansas River. The mile numbers in part II refer to the river itself, but they can, with varying degrees of accuracy, also be used to locate points of interest along Highways 24, 285, 291, and 50.

DEFINITION OF TERMS

"River left" and "river right" refer to the left and right sides of the river when facing downstream.

The adjectives "low," "medium," "high" and "very high" used to describe the river's volume correspond roughly to the following flow rates in cubic feet per second (cfs):

low	below 1,500 cfs
medium	1,500 to 3,000 cfs
high	3,000 to 4,500 cfs
very high	above 4,500 cfs

For current flow rates call one of the local rafting companies listed in appendix 2. Remember that the flow volume in the upper parts of the river are often less than

PART I

GETTING TO KNOW
THE ARKANSAS

1. THE RIVER'S STORY

The river which carved the magnificent canyons of Lake, Chaffee and Fremont Counties begins as a modest trout stream near the Continental Divide just below Fremont Pass. By the time the Arkansas reaches the Mississippi, most of its water has been drained for irrigation on the plains.

But while it's still in the mountains, the Arkansas is lively and constant, dropping 5,000 feet in its first 125 miles. Clyde Byron Davis, in his book *The Arkansas*, describes it as "one of the most rambunctious of American rivers, one of the longest; at times one of the most treacherous. Surely no American river has seen more varied or more incredible history in the making."

HISTORICAL OVERVIEW

The first European to see the point where the Arkansas leaves the mountains (near present-day Canon City) was probably the Spaniard Juan de Ulibarri in 1706. Apparently, he arrived during the late spring runoff when the river takes on the ruddy color of mud, for he named it *Napestle*, an Indian word meaning "red water."

The modern name Arkansas comes from the Les Arkansas Indians who lived in what is now Oklahoma and Arkansas. These are the states through which the river passes after leaving Colorado and Kansas.

Zebulon Pike was the first white man to explore the rugged upper portion of the Arkansas in 1806. Thirty years later, Captain John C. Fremont retraced much of Pike's route. The upper Arkansas was probably also visited by French fur traders until hat styles changed from beaver to silk around 1840.

During 1859, gold fever spread west into the Arkansas Valley from Colorado's Front Range. In that year, a prospector was so thrilled with the pile of gold dust he panned from a sidestream near the Arkansas' headwaters that he yelled, "This here is California." The stream valley thus became known as California Gulch and experienced one of the West's greatest immigrations of miners. A mining camp was quickly erected and christened Oro City. Each summer, Oro City is temporarily recreated for the tourists.

After a few years, the California Gulch gold dwindled. Then in 1878, a rich percentage of silver was discovered in the abundant lead carbonate sand which the miners had previously regarded as a nuisance. Before long, most of the Oro City settlers moved down to the mouth of California Gulch, and the boom town of Leadville was born. Over the years, other valuable metals have been wrung from the rich ores in the high country bordering the Arkansas.

The story of mining along the upper Arkansas is intertwined with the history of railroading. Hauling the output of the Leadville silver mines over the Mosquito Mountains by wagon was grueling and expensive. A railroad was needed, and the river canyons provided a natural corridor for the track. However, building a railroad next to the Arkansas proved not only to be a challenging engineering feat but one of the west's most bitter episodes of violence. (See miles 34.2 and 99.6 in chapter 4.)

To someone driving along the Arkansas on Highways 50 or 285, ranching and hay farming are the most visible occupations. Chris Madson, writing in *Audubon* magazine, described a portion of the area perfectly: "You won't find a valley that fits the video dreams of an urban cowboy better than the country between Buena Vista and Salida. Where there is water, the fields have the contours of a well-fed Hereford. The farmhouses are fresh-painted and shaded by elm and cottonwood. The fences are taut, and the alfalfa and sleek horseflesh and livestock it supports would drive a Kentucky colonel into early retirement."

The upper Arkansas Valley has known a series of booms and busts caused mainly by the oscillating demand for its minerals. Recently, the region's economy has taken a nose dive due to the decline of the Climax Molybdenum Mine near Leadville. For-sale signs have been popping up in front yards like flags on the Fourth of July. But many residents are reluctant to leave the majestic beauty of their mountains and canyons, and are looking for other ways to make a living. The surrounding ski areas have helped somewhat. But the lion's share of Colorado's tourist income comes during the summer, and the Upper Arkansas Valley residents want to increase their cut by seeking help from their old friend—the river. Commercial rafting is now one of the area's most important industries, and together with the scenery, it provides the main magnet for summer tourists.

A recent article in a summer publication put out by the

Mountain Mail, a Salida newspaper, asked "Will success spoil the Arkansas?" In 1987, 62 companies received permits from the Bureau of Land Management (BLM) to run raft trips on the Arkansas. Since 1983, the river has seen an average annual increase of 21 percent in commercial raft use. The number of paying customers using BLM land along the river has risen from 40,794 in 1980 to 89,114 in 1986. When this is considered along with the estimated 22,000 private boaters (in 1986), access to Colorado's favorite river may soon have to be curtailed. Otherwise, put-in and take-out points will become overcrowded, and the impact on shore from lunch and camping stops will be too great, not to mention the safety problems associated with scores of boats on a narrow river.

Commercial outfitters on the Arkansas are well aware that rafting, like mining, is a fickle business. Whenever there's a boating death, the number of reservations plummet despite the fact that the risk to life and limb is greater on the highways paralleling the Arkansas than on the river itself. Also, most of the deaths that have occurred on the Arkansas have been private rather than commercial boaters. "No distinction is made [by the media] between the trained boatmen around here and the bubble-headed misadventurer who is in peril when he fills the bathtub," observes Ray James, a reporter for the *Mountain Mail*.

Community leaders are hoping to attract light, clean industries that can put people to work and counteract slumps in the whitewater rafting and tourist markets. For most residents in the Upper Arkansas Valley, the word "clean" is critical—especially in regard to the river, which passes so close to so many doors. This was true in the 1930s when silt and other pollutants from California Gulch placer mines wiped out virtually the entire Arkansas fish population between Leadville and Salida, and 350 local sportsmen confronted the problem by forming the Chaffee County Fish and Game Association. And it's true today, as sulfuric acid from the old mines near Leadville is leaching mercury, cadmium, lead, selenium and other heavy metals into the river. For many people in the Arkansas Valley, the river is a treasured resource, and threats to its purity are regarded as threats to their wholesome lifestyle.

READING THE ROCKS

The upper Arkansas is a true high-country river. Its steep rocky gradient makes for excellent whitewater, and the mountainous scenery contains some fascinating geology. A lot happened here in the last 600 million years. Great seas advanced and retreated. Mountains rose up and were worn away. Volcanoes erupted and glaciers gnawed at the land. Today, the Arkansas cuts through the vestiges of these and other great events.

Understanding the rocks and how they were formed isn't as easy along the Arkansas as it is in places like the Grand Canyon of the Colorado where the earth's history is exposed in a layer cake-like sequence of strata. The geology seen from an Arkansas River boat is less straightforward but much more dramatic due to the slow violence of mountain building.

Before discussing the origin of the Arkansas Valley's landscape, let's review some basic geology. As you may remember from school, there are three basic rock types: igneous, sedimentary and metamorphic.

- IGNEOUS rocks are solidified molten material. The molten material is called magma if it lies deep underground, or lava if it comes onto or near the surface.

- SEDIMENTARY rocks are fomed from sediments such as loose rocks, sand, silt or animal remains.

- METAMORPHIC rocks have undergone a drastic change in their crystal structure caused by intense heat, pressure or chemical action. Before the change they may have been igneous, sedimentary or some other kind of metamorphic rock.

The solid part of the earth's crust is composed of bedrock which can be either igneous, metamorphic or sedimentary. In many places along the Arkansas, the bedrock is exposed for our examination. In other places, it is covered with loose material which may have been derived directly from the underlying bedrock or transported from somewhere else either by the river, its sidestreams or ice-age glaciers.

Cracks form in the bedrock, especially in and around areas of mountain building. The cracks are called joints. If movement occurs along a joint it is called a fault. The Arkansas Valley area is full of joints and faults. Certain major faults may cause sharp changes in the scenery. These have been given names. For example, the Pleasant Valley Fault is responsible for the prominent cliff face north of the river along Highway 50 between Coaldale and Cotopaxi. (See miles 67.3 and 72 in part II, chapter 4.)

Some of the rocks along the Arkansas are thought to be

TABLE 1 GEOLOGIC HISTORY

era	period	epoch	age in millions of years	major geologic events in Colorado	geologic formations along the Arkansas
CENOZOIC					
	Quaternary		0–1	Three distinct glaciations.	Glacial stream deposits.
	Tertiary	Pliocene	12	Rockies uplifted 3,000-5,000 ft. with erosion and deposition in valleys.	Dry Union Form. Rio Grande Rift
		Miocene	25		Sangre de Cristo Mountains
		Oligocene	38	Extensive volcanism.	Buffalo Peaks Wall Mountain Volcanics 39 Mile Volcanic Field
		Eocene	54		Sawatch Uplift
		Paleocene	65	Laramide Orogeny Most of modern Rockies formed.	

Era	Period		Event	Formation
MESOZOIC	Cretaceous	135	Sea covers Colorado then recedes.	Pierre Shale Niobrara Limestone Dakota Sandstone
	Jurassic	200	Desert, then sea advances and climate moistens.	Morrison Formation
	Triassic	240	Floodplains and deserts.	
PALEOZOIC	Permian	280	Floodplains and deserts. Erosion of Ancestral Rockies continues.	Sangre de Cristo Sandstone and Shale
	Pennsyl-vanian	325	Colorado Orogeny Ancestral Rockies formed and partly eroded into surrounding ocean.	Minturn Sandstone, Shale and Limestone
	Missis-sippian	370	Sea covers much of western North America.	Leadville Limestone

Period	Age	Description	Rock Formations
Devonian	415	Colorado partially covered by ocean.	Chaffee Dolomite, Sandstone, Limestone
Silurian	445	Shallow sea probably covers the state.	No Silurian deposits along Arkansas.
Ordovician	515	Sea deepens, recedes, and deepens again.	Freemont Dolomite, Harding Quartzite, Manitou Dolomite
Cambrian	570	Sea advances eastward depositing beach sand.	Sawatch Quartzite (limited exposure along Arkansas)
PRECAMBRIAN	1,000–5,000	Repeated mountain building and erosion ending with a long period of erosion called the Lipalian Interval.	Hard, crystalline granite, schist and gneiss on most moutain summits and in most Arkansas River Canyons.

1.75 billion years old. The usual adjectives for great age like "old" and "ancient" pall at such a span. So geologists have invented a number of more precise terms for time (table 1). In this book, we'll get by with just six: the Precambrian, Paleozoic, Mesozoic and Cenozoic Eras and the Tertiary and Quaternary Periods. For completeness, table 1 lists most of the geologic time scale including the epochs of the Tertiary Period.

Rocks of the Precambrian Era are the oldest—at least 570 million years. They represent 80 to 85 percent of the Earth's history. Most of their existence is spent deep within the Earth's crust where they often become so metamorphosed by heat and pressure that they give us little information. Precambrian rocks may be exposed when they are brought to the surface, as in orogeny (mountain building), or when the overlaying material is eroded away as in canyon cutting.

Above the Precambrian basement complex are rocks of the Paleozoic, Mesozoic and Cenozoic Eras. As you might expect, most of the rocks from these more recent eras are sedimentary, but some are igneous and a small number are metamorphic.

The boundary between the oldest Paleozoic rocks and the underlying Precambrian basement complex is the surface which remained after the Precambrian rocks were worn down by erosion, but before overlaying layers were deposited. It represents a large blank spot in our knowledge known as the Lipalian Interval.

Each era is divided into periods. These can be tedious for the layman, so we'll concern ourselves with only the two periods of the most recent era, the Cenozoic. These are the Tertiary and the Quaternary. The Rockies began their rise about 65 or 70 million years ago at the start of the Tertiary Period. The Quaternary, which is still going on, extends back about two million years. Glaciers periodically filled many of Colorado's mountain valleys during the Quaternary, and the polar ice cap crept all the way down to Montana.

To understand how the Rocky Mountains got here, some familiarity with the concept of plate tectonics is helpful. This theory was to geology in the 1960s what Darwin's theory of natural selection was to biology in the 1860s. According to the plate tectonic theory, the Earth's crust is composed of a dozen or so plates. The 60-mile-thick plates move as a result of heat and other disturbances from the inner earth. The plates are separated from each other by oceanic ridges and trenches. At the ridges, the plates move apart and lava wells up from the Earth's interior to form new plate material. This causes the sea floor to "spread." At the trenches, the edge of one plate slides beneath the edge of another and is eventually re-melted. Thus, a plate is continually moving from ridge to trench.

The Rockies represent a weak spot in the North American plate, where it crumbled and broke into great mountain ranges running in a north-south direction. This was apparently related to stresses from two intense periods of sea floor spreading along the mid-Atlantic Ridge. One such period occurred about 300 million years ago and caused the late Paleozoic Colorado Orogeny. This formed

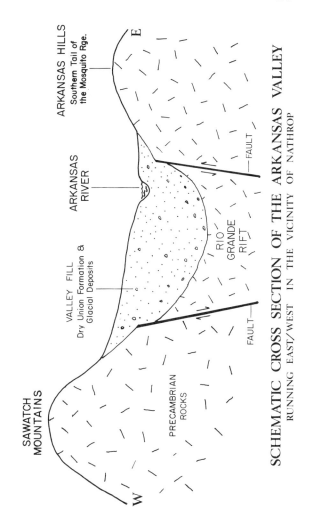

SCHEMATIC CROSS SECTION OF THE ARKANSAS VALLEY
RUNNING EAST/WEST IN THE VICINITY OF NATHROP

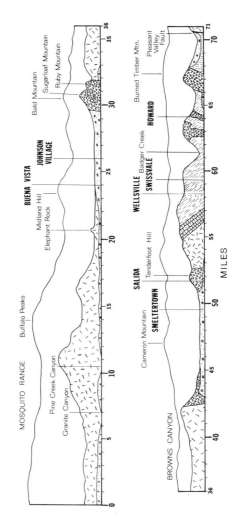

DIAGRAMMATIC SECTION

SHOWING THE GEOLOGY ALONG THE ARKANSAS RIVER

Looking East (North of Salida) & Looking North (East of Salida)

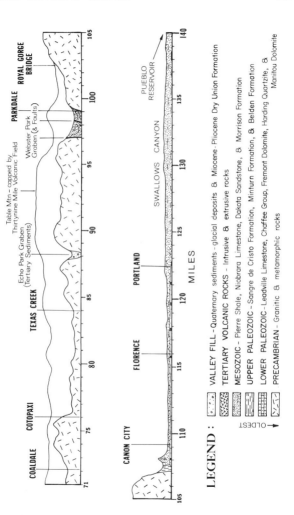

LEGEND :

VALLEY FILL – Quaternary sediments – glacial deposits & Miocene - Pliocene Dry Union Formation

TERTIARY VOLCANIC ROCKS – Intrusive & extrusive rocks

MESOZOIC – Pierre Shale, Niobrara Limestone, Dakota Sandstone, & Morrison Formation

UPPER PALEOZOIC – Sangre de Cristo Formation, Minturn Formation, & Belden Formation

LOWER PALEOZOIC – Leadville Limestone, Chaffee Group, Fremont Dolomite, Harding Quartzite, & Manitou Dolomite

PRECAMBRIAN – Granitic & metamorphic rocks

OLDEST ⟶

MILES

COALDALE COTOPAXI TEXAS CREEK PARKDALE ROYAL GORGE BRIDGE

Table Mtn - capped by Thirtynine Mile Volcanic Field

Echo Park Graben (Tertiary Sediments)

Webster Park Graben (& Faults)

71 75 80 85 90 95 100 105

CANON CITY FLORENCE PORTLAND SWALLOWS CANYON PUEBLO RESERVOIR

105 110 115 120 125 130 135 140

the Ancestral Rocky Mountains which have since been
eroded out of existence. The other episode of sea floor
spreading caused the Laramide Orogeny of the early Tertiary period. This occurred between 70 and 45 million years
ago and created the basic structure of the modern Rockies.

GEOLOGIC HISTORY OF
THE ARKANSAS VALLEY

During the early Tertiary Laramide Orogeny, the Precambrian foundation of the Earth's crust swelled into an
enormous hump called the Sawatch Uplift in what is now
Chaffee, Lake and eastern Gunnison Counties. Later in the
Tertiary, beginning about 30 million years ago, the center
of the hump weakened and cracked on two sides to form a
separate block as the Rockies experienced a renewed
uplifting. While most of the Sawatch hump rose up, this
central block remained low to form the Rio Grande Rift, a
depression running north and south from Leadville to
Mexico. At its northern end, the elevated sides of the hump
became the Mosquito Range to the east and the great
Sawatch Range to the west. Streams flowed out of the
mountains and merged on the central rift valley to form the
Arkansas River.

Recent findings suggest that the Arkansas once followed the Rio Grande Rift straight south into the San Luis
Valley where it merged with the Rio Grande River. What
is believed to be an old river channel, filled with material
ejected from the San Juan Mountain volcanic area, has
been found near Poncha Pass. But today, the Arkansas
takes a hard left near Salida into the low area between the

Sangre de Cristo Mountains and the southern tail of the Mosquito Range Foothills (also known as the Arkansas Hills). It then flows between the Thirty-nine Mile Volcanic Field to the north and the head of the Wet Mountains to the south before passing through the Royal Gorge Plateau and out onto the Great Plains. Eventually it joins the Mississippi River after traveling 1,450 miles from its headwaters at the foot of Mount Arkansas.

Throughout much of the Tertiary Period, the Arkansas Valley region was blasted by vulcanism. Ash and rock fragments were ejected from vents, and lava poured onto the surface. The Twin Mountains, known as the Buffalo Peaks in the Mosquito Range east of the river, are eroded remnants of one such volcanic episode. Other examples of volcanic activity along the Arkansas occur at Rainbow Rock (mile 31), Ruby Mountain (mile 31.6), the southern end of Brown's Canyon (mile 41.2), Tenderfoot Hill in Salida (mile 51.7), Badger Creek in Howard (mile 61.4) and in certain parts of the Lower Arkansas Canyon (mile 84.8) and the Royal Gorge (mile 100.8).

As recently as 10,000 years ago, massive ice sheets covered much of North America. During the three Quaternary ice ages known to affect Colorado, the great continental glaciers did not extend to the southern Rockies. However, valley glaciers did fill the upper drainages of the Sawatch and Sangre de Cristo Ranges down to an altitude of about 8,000 feet. The slowly moving ice scoured the valleys into the U shapes which characterize glacial action. In contrast, the valleys of the southern Mosquito Mountains didn't see many glaciers because of their lower altitude and smaller precipitation levels. They thus retained the V shape typical of stream erosion.

The valley glaciers from the Sawatch Mountains carried great quantities of rocky debris toward the river. Some of the debris fell from the cliffsides and some was plucked from the surface of the mountains by the creeping ice. At the terminus of each glacier, the ice melted but the glacier did not retreat because more ice was continually added at its head. And so for hundreds of years, rocks, gravel, sand and silt were moved downhill, conveyor belt style, and dropped at the foot of the glaciers to form giant hills called terminal moraines.

The masses of sediment carried by the Sawatch Mountain glaciers and their streams of meltwater pushed the Arkansas' course so far eastward that it flowed directly above the west edge of the Mosquito Range's Precambrian core where it cut the hard rock canyons between Leadville and Salida. Likewise, from Howard to Coaldale, glacial sediment from the Sangre de Cristo Mountains shoved the river northward across Pleasant Valley and up against the southern boundary of the Arkansas Hills.

For some, the length of the intervals in table 1 and the ages given for the rocks along the Arkansas may conflict with personal beliefs about the creation of the universe. But the nature and sequence of the geologic events is hard to debate. And the agents of geologic change are thought to have worked in the primeval world just as they do today— very slowly, with occasional catastrophes like earthquakes, landslides, flash floods and volcanoes.

LIFE IN THE HIGH COUNTRY

It might be difficult for a whitewater-drenched river traveler to realize that the Upper Arkansas flows through a kind of desert. Most of the moisture in the prevailing westerlies is trapped by the Sawatch Mountains, leaving little for the foothills and valley floor. The yearly snowfall in central Chaffee County is less than 50 inches, while in the mountains only 20 miles away it may be well over 100 inches. Even during the summer wet season, less than two inches of rain falls per month on the Arkansas Valley, which is, in fact, so dry and sunny that it's known as Colorado's "banana belt."

Unlike a true desert, much of the land along the runnable portions of the Arkansas is forest covered. But most of the trees are arid weather specialists—capable of surviving droughts and quickly absorbing their meager share of moisture before it evaporates or runs off through the coarse soil.

The upper reaches of the Arkansas are moister than the lower sections because as air rises and cools (three to five degrees for every thousand feet), it loses its ability to hold water. Thus, rain and snow fall in increasing amounts at progressively higher altitudes.

These variations in temperature and moisture cause variations in plant life. If you could travel from the Arkansas' headwaters all the way past Canon City to the Great Plains, you'd notice a gradual change in the dominant trees and bushes. These changes correspond roughly to specific life zones which ecologists have defined for the Colorado mountains (altitudes are approximate):

- Plains Zone—up to about 6,000 feet—Dry grasslands with occasional shrubs. Few trees except along watercourses.
- Foothills Zone—6,000 to 8,000 feet—Open forests of ponderosa pine on sunny, dry, south-facing slopes and Douglas fir in moister locations such as shaded north-facing slopes. These are intermixed with extensive open areas of grass and shrubs interspersed with pygmy forests of pinyon and juniper.
- Montane Zone—8,000 to 10,000 feet—Forests of ponderosa pine and Douglas fir occur in the lower limits and are denser than in the foothills. Engelmann spruce, limber pine, bristlecone pine and subalpine fir are found in the upper limits. Also, stands of aspen and lodgepole pine develop after forest fires or in areas of past disturbance.
- Subalpine Zone—10,000 to 11,500 feet—Dense, moist forests of Engelmann spruce and subalpine fir. Also, lodgepole pine and aspen at lower limits and limber and bristlecone pine at upper limits and along exposed ridges.
- Alpine Zone—above 11,500 feet—No tree growth due to severe cold, high winds and a very short growing season. Mostly low shrubs and perennial herbs.

Don't let this classification fool you into thinking that the correlation between plant life and altitude is always consistent, because it isn't. Patches of the treeless plains may frequently exist in dry, sunlit areas above 6,000 feet. Likewise, trees which are common in the high mountains may be found in moist bottom lands of the lower foothills.

The mile-by-mile descriptions in chapter 4 deal primarily with the montane, foothills and plains life zones. The navigable portions of the Arkansas don't flow through the alpine and subalpine zones, but they are visible from the river. The alpine zone appears as the treeless crowns on the high mountains. The dark green bands below the tree line are the thick subalpine forests of Engelmann spruce and subalpine fir. Light green patches are aspen groves, and medium green indicates stands of lodgepole pine.

The cold-adapted vegetation of the high Rockies is very similar to that of the northwoods and tundra barrens in Canada and Alaska. And, as in the north country, snow is present in Colorado's alpine and subalpine life zones during most of the year. Much of the Arkansas' water originates from the abundant snow melting in these two environments. Should they become overly developed, their ability to hold water would be hampered, thus increasing the risk of lowland flooding.

The plant communities immediately next to the river and its sidestreams are often very different from those on the surrounding hillsides. These areas are called riparian, meaning "adjacent to water." Although riparian environments are limited to the moist ribbons of land bordering streams, lakes and rivers, they are vital to the survival of practically all of the state's wildlife. Riparian plant communities are often quite dense. They may contain three times the number of plant species as the adjacent hillsides, thus providing abundant food, shelter and nesting sites for animals. In some parts of Colorado, approximately 50

percent of the birds nest in riparian communities while up
to 80 percent of the mammals, reptiles, and amphibians
make their homes there. Riverside plants are also necessary
for erosion control. But all too often, pristine river frontage
is converted into restaurants, resorts, highways, sub-
divisions and overgrazed pastures.

Riparian habitats are widest where the river's gradient
is most gentle. Steep-sided canyons, like Browns and the
Royal Gorge, lack the flood plains necessary for the growth
of willows, alders, cottonwoods and other moisture-loving
species.

High-country animals are less restricted than plants by
environmental conditions. Mule deer, one of the more
commonly seen game animals along the Arkansas, are
found practically anywhere from the plains to tree line,
depending on the season. Elk, or Wapiti, were once more
wide-ranging than they are today. Elk sightings along the
river are very unusual. Like many animals, bighorn sheep
have lost much of their range to civilization. However, the
shy bighorn is seen with some regularity along the Arkansas (miles 40.6 and 89.4 in chapter 4).

Smaller animals which may be seen in the Arkansas
Valley are chipmunks, tassel-eared (abert) squirrels, red
squirrels, weasels, beavers, muskrats, skunks, cottontail
rabbits, jackrabbits, bats, fence lizards, gopher snakes,
smooth green snakes and an occasional rattlesnake.

BIRDS ALONG THE ARKANSAS

No wild animals are easier to observe than the birds. It's unlikely that you'll see a deer drinking along shore or a bighorn sheep trotting up a rocky hillside. But the chances are very good that you'll see a water ouzel slip beneath the water in search of food, or a flock of blackbirds harass a large raven, or a great blue heron slam its saber-shaped bill into an unsuspecting minnow.

Using binoculars from a moving river boat is difficult. But birdwatching along the Arkansas can still be productive because of the richness of life near water. The best time to see birds is during the spring when they're busy with reproduction and early and late in the day when they generally feed.

In the following species descriptions L stands for the head-to-tail length. The wingspan, W, is also given for some species. The mile numbers in parentheses refer to entries in part II.

MALLARD (*Anas platyrhynchos*). L 16", W 36", Male—green head and rusty breast. Female—mottled brown. Both with blue wing patches.

RED-BREASTED MERGANSER (*Mergus serrator*). L 16", W 26". Bill thinner than in other ducks and with serrated edges for catching fish. Male—green head. Female—reddish brown head. (mile 42.5)

TURKEY VULTURE (*Cathartes aura*). L 25", W 72". When soaring, holds wings on a slight backswept arch rather than straight across as do hawks and eagles. Often in groups.

GREAT BLUE HERON (*Ardes herodias*). L 38", W 70". Wades the shallows in search of fish. Legs hang down after takeoff. (Swallows Canyon, mile 123)

KESTRAL OR SPARROW HAWK (*Falco sparverius*). L 8.5", W 21". Small falcon, often hovers. Rusty back is diagnostic. (mile 42.5)

RED-TAILED HAWK (*Buteo jamaicensis*). L 18", W 48". Plumage variable but red tail and dark belly band usually present.

GOLDEN EAGLE (*Aquila chrysaetos*). L 32", W 78". Rare. Adult dark brown. Immature—white tail band and wing patches.

SPOTTED SANDPIPER (*Actitis macularia*). L 6.25". Grayish brown above, white below. Bobs tail as it stands on shore. Flies close to the water with rapid beats of pointed wings.

Mallard

Red-Breasted
Merganser

Turkey Vulture

Great Blue Heron

Kestral or Sparrow Hawk

Red-Tailed Hawk

CALIFORNIA GULL (*Larus californicus*). L 17", W 52".
May stray from the dump southwest of Browns Canyon.
Gray and white with long pointed wings.

ROCK DOVE OR PIGEON (*Columba livia*). L 13.5".
White rump and dark tail band (except in white birds).
Glides with wings swept back. Thick body with rounded
contours. Often seen around the railroad bridge at the beginning of Browns Canyon.

MOURNING DOVE (*Zenaidura macroura*). L 10.5".
Slim, grayish brown body and long tapering tail bordered
with white. Rounded contours like pigeon.

GREAT HORNED OWL (*Bubo virginianus*). L 20", W
55". This largest owl has "ears" and a huge wingspan. Look
for it in the alders and cottonwoods above and below
Browns Canyon.

WHITE-THROATED SWIFT (*Aeronautes saxatalis*). L
6.5", W 14". Distinguished from swallows with which they
are often found by black and white plumage and larger size.
Soars rapidly around high cliffs.

BROAD-TAILED HUMMINGBIRD (*Selasphorus
platycercus*). L 3.75". Humming sound from rapid wing-
beats often heard without ever seeing this fast little bird.
Long, thin bill for slurping nectar from tubular flowers.
(mile 32.5)

golden Eagle

Spotted Sandpiper

California Gull

Rock Dove or Pigeon

Mourning Dove

great-Horned Owl

BELTED KINGFISHER (*Megaceryle alcyon*). L 12".
Large crested head and heavy bill. Blue-gray plumage with
reddish chest band in female. Shy. (mile 42.5)

LEWIS WOODPECKER (*Asyndesmus lewis*). L 9". Red
face and light front stand out against dark green (almost
black) wings and tail. Slow flight with even flapping. (mile
65.3)

FLICKER (*Colaptes auratus*). L 11". White spot appears
at base of tail during flight which consists of series of
down—arched glides separated by bursts of flapping. Very
common. Spends more time on the ground than other
woodpeckers. (mile 65.3)

VIOLET-GREEN SWALLOW (*Tachycineta thalassina*).
L 4.75". Green back with white belly and white side
patches that almost meet on the lower back. Swallows fly
rapidly and erratically, catching insects in midair.

BARN SWALLOW (*Hirundo rustica*). L 6". Blue and orange. Only swallow with a forked tail. Usually not far from
buildings. (mile 63.8)

CLIFF SWALLOW (*Petrochelidon pyrrhonota*). L 5".
Markings similar to barn swallow but has orange rump and
squared-off tail. (miles 42.5 and 123)

White- Throated Swift

Broad- Tailed Hummingbird

Belted King fisher

Lewis Woodpecker

Flicker

Violet- Green Swallow

CLARK'S NUTCRACKER (*Nucifraga columbiana*). L 11". Black and white plumage of this jay is distinctive.

CROW (*Corvus brachyrhynchos*). L 17". All black. Flaps more than hawks. Tail with straight edges. Call is a "caw."

RAVEN (*Corvus corax*). L 21". Larger than crows with a heavier bill and diamond-shaped tail.

BLACK-BILLED MAGPIE (*Pica pica*). L 18". Very long tail. Harsh call like that of other members of the crow and jay family. Black, white and irridescent green (not always visible).

DIPPER OR WATER OUZEL (*Cinclus mexicanus*). L 5.75". Slate-colored. Flies close to the water. Bobs up and down when standing on shore. Found from the plains to timberline. Relatively tame. Large igloo-shaped nests of plant material are built on rock faces just above water line. Sometimes land on water and then submerge to pick insect larva from shallow bottoms. Ouzels are regarded as mascots by the local river guides.

ROBIN (*Turdus migratorius*). L 8.5". The orange breast of this wide-ranging bird is diagnostic. Those along the Arkansas may leave for the winter but are replaced by migrants from the north.

Barn Swallow

Cliff Swallow + Nest

Clark's Nutcracker

Crow

Raven

Black-Billed Magpie

TOWNSEND'S SOLITAIRE (*Myadestes townsendi*). L 6.5". Upright stance and light wing markings. Common in ponderosa pine and Douglas fir of Browns Canyon where they are darker than those pictured in the field guides. At first glance, might be mistaken for a small, thin robin.

STARLING (*Sturnus vulgaris*). L 6". Shorter tail than other black-colored birds. Yellow bill during spring and summer.

BREWER'S BLACKBIRD (*Euphagus cyanocephalus*). L 8". The common blackbird in the Arkansas Valley. Male may have purplish sheen on head. Female brown.

WESTERN TANAGER (*Piranga ludoviciana*). 6.25". Male—red head, yellow body and black wings. Female—yellow with black wings and greenish head and back. In pine and Douglas Fir.

YELLOW WARBLER (*Dendroica petechia*). L 4". Small, all yellow insect eater mistakenly called a canary. (mile 32.5)

Dipper or Water Ouzel

Robin

Townsend's Solitaire

Starling

Brewer's Blackbird

Western Tanager

RED-WINGED BLACKBIRD (*Agelaius phoeniceus*). L
7.25". Male—all black with red shoulder patches. Female
and immature—heavy brown streaks. (mile 63.3)

AMERICAN GOLDFINCH (*Spinus tristis*). L 4.25". A
yellow bird, approximately the same size as the yellow
warbler but with black wings and a stouter bill for seed
cracking (mile 32.5).

Yellow Warbler

Red-Winged Blackbird

American Goldfinch

LIFE IN THE RIVER

Fish are occasionally seen darting across the river bottom. At least 29 different species of fish have been recorded in the portion of the Arkansas covered by this book (table 2). A number of these are introduced species.

Table 3 lists those flies which fishermen have had the greatest success with on the Arkansas. Most of the fish caught are brown trout, the only Arkansas trout that reproduces in the river itself. Browns were originally brought over from Europe. Rainbow trout, which originated on the West Coast, are caught in much smaller numbers. All the rainbows in the Arkansas are either introduced by stocking or escape from local trout farms.

TABLE 2—ARKANSAS RIVER FISHES

(Species collected by the Colorado Department of Wildlife during the Arkansas River Threatened Fishes Survey, 1979–1981. The number collected follows each name).

Brook trout	2	*	Carp	445	**
Rainbow trout	3		Tench	5	**
Brown trout	27		Channel catfish	107	**
White sucker	1,195		Black bullhead	578	**
Longnose sucker	121		Plains killifish	6,103	**
Creek chub	381	**	Mosquitofish	53	**
Flathead chub	2,020		Smallmouth bass	2	**
Sand shiner	10,674	**	Largemouth bass	3	**
Red shiner	4,351	**	Green sunfish	1,503	**
Bigmouth shiner	73	**	Orangespotted sunfish	49	**

Flathead minnow	4,398	**	White crappie	61	**
Suckermouth minnow	680	**	Walleye	15	**
Longnose dace	1,120	*	Arkansas darter	780	**
Southern redbelly dace	28	**	Brook stickleback	105	**

Stoneroller   4,072   **

Totals   29 species   38,954 specimens

* Fish occurring between Granite and Canon City.
** Fish occurring between Canyon City and the Pueblo Reservoir.
Fish with no asterick—between Granite and the Pueblo Reservoir.

TABLE 3—POPULAR FISHING FLIES USED ON THE ARKANSAS

dry flies	size	time of year
Blue Dun	14 & 16	mid-April
Elk Hair Caddis	12–16	all summer
Royal Wolf	16	all summer
Midge Adult	2024	December–March (early afternoon)

nymphs	size	time of year
Yellow Stonefly	8	all year
Dark Stonefly	8	all year
Olive Caddis	12, 14 or 16	all year
Midge Nymph	20–24	December–March (early afternoon)

The major food item for fish in the Arkansas River is insect larva. Flies, caddisflies, stoneflies, mayflies and many other insects lay their eggs in the water. The eggs hatch into aquatic larvae which eventually metamorphose into flying adults, some of which may live no more than a few days.

Although these aquatic invertebrates vary greatly in appearance, there are certain characteristics which they may share. Many have hooks, suckers or some other means of attaching themselves to the rocks and gravel on the bottom (sandy bottoms in rivers and streams support almost no aquatic insects). Their streamlined bodies offer a minimum of resistance to the current. Many stream-dwelling insects have flatter shapes than their counterparts in ponds and lakes, enabling them to crawl under stones. Most river creatures will consistently orient themselves with their heads upstream, and many invertebrates living in running water will always try to cling to whatever object is at hand even when placed in a jar of water.

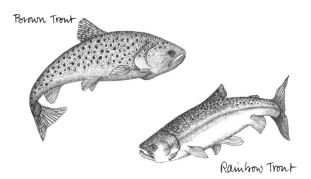

Brown Trout

Rainbow Trout

The most easily observed aquatic animals in the Arkansas are the caddisfly larvae. Almost any rock pulled from a shallow bottom will have at least one of these odd creatures clinging to it. But what you first see isn't the animal. It's the half-inch-long case which the soft-bodied larva builds around itself by gluing together bits of sediment. Each caddisfly species builds its own characteristic case. Some use tiny bits of plant material. Others use gravel and grains of sand. If you hold a rock covered with caddisfly cases out of the water long enough, the larvae will eventually stick out their heads and crawl around, dragging their homes behind them. When a caddisfly larva is fully grown it attaches its case to the rock and closes off the opening. It then changes into the pupa stage, chews its way out of the case, floats up to the water's surface, undergoes a final molt into an adult caddisfly, and flies away. As they float on the surface of the water, they are easy prey for hungry fish.

Although algae grows on the rocks, rivers like the Upper Arkansas are generally too swift for large aquatic plants. Thus, much of the food for the small aquatic animals falls from the trees and bushes or is washed in from the land.

2   BOATING ON THE ARKANSAS

The recent surge in boating traffic on the Arkansas River between Leadville and Pueblo is due not only to outstanding whitewater and striking scenery but also to accessibility. The starting points for many trips on the Arkansas can be reached in an hour by car from Colorado Springs and in less than three hours from Denver. Furthermore, the abundant put-in and take-out points along the Arkansas make it possible to choose from a variety of short trips ranging in difficulty from the gentle canoeable water in Swallows Canyon to the highly technical whitewater of Rapids One Through Six. Since most of the river is paralleled by paved roads, car shuttles are easy.

The Arkansas' long boating season adds to its appeal. A peak runoff of approximately 1 to 6,000 cubic feet per second normally occurs from early June to mid-July. Many sections are passable from May through September depending on the depth of the winter snowpack, its rate of melting, the type of craft being used and the release schedule from Twin Lakes Reservoir below Leadville.

SAFE BOATING
With bigger crowds have come bigger problems and a greater likelihood for mishaps even on the best-run commercial trips. The new regulations for river running set forth

by the Colorado State Division of Parks and Outdoor Recreation may or may not make a difference but at least they're prodding everyone toward a greater safety consciousness. The half dozen boating deaths on the Arkansas from 1981 to 1986 have shown that this is a river to be taken seriously.

To this end, brief descriptions are provided for technical boulder fields and rapids rated class III and above. But the river changes constantly. Sandbars evolve, suckholes fill in and new rocks enter from slides and flash floods creating new pour-overs and reflective waves. Plus, during high water there's always the chance of the boatman's nightmare becoming a reality—a "strainer" tree wedged across a narrow channel, pinning boat and passengers against a strong current.

The point is, if you're not familiar with the Arkansas, don't let this book be your sole source of information about how to run it. Ask questions. Call one or two of the commercial outfitters in appendix 2 to learn the locations of any new danger spots. Make sure you talk to somebody who knows specifically about the run you plan to take. A rafting company's head river guide is often a friendly source.

Neither should this book be used as a substitute for boating experience. Rafters and kayakers on the Arkansas should be able to evaluate their own ability and equipment in relation to the following International rating scale:

Class I   Easy

              Small waves
              No obstacles

Class II   Medium
           Moderate rapids with small drops
           Clear passages
           Requires decent equipment

Class III   Difficult
           Expertise in maneuvering needed
           Requires good operator and boat
           Scouting usually needed

Class IV   Very difficult
           Large irregular waves
           Fast water
           Assorted hazards
           Precise maneuvering required
           Scouting mandatory first time
           Demands very experienced and competent guide and excellent equipment

Class V   Extremely difficult
           Steep gradient
           Inspection absolutely necessary
           Requires the most proficient of operators and highest quality equipment

Class VI   Ultimate limit of navigability
           Loss of life possible
           Some consider such rapids unrunnable

Class VII Never been run successfully

All but a few of the runs described in chapter 3 have class III water, some have class IV and several contain class V.

When two classes are given for a single rapid, the

second usually refers to the condition in high water (above 3,000 cfs) because high water is generally thought to hold the greatest risks. But in a rocky river like the Arkansas, low water has its own special problems: oars turning into missiles after hitting rocks and popping off their pins, passengers in the back of a raft crunching into a rowing frame, swimmers hitting rocks, rafts wrapping around large boulders and the obvious increase in wear and tear on the boats.

Scout frequently during your first runs through any trip or after significant changes in the water level. Scouting is generally easiest on the side of the river with the railroad but bear in mind that trespassing is illegal on railroad property. Watch out for fast freights—especially on curves. Sound is not always a reliable warning of the approach of a train or one of the small work cars. The Denver and Rio Grande Railroad has been very cooperative in helping with search-and-rescue operations on the river so please be mindful of their concerns.

Unless stated otherwise, the following descriptions and suggestions are geared towards 14- to 18-foot inflatable rafts. It is assumed that kayakers can fit through tighter spots due to their smaller size and greater maneuverability. Thus, kayakers will often have more options for a safe line of passage through a rapid than those described here.

MIND YOUR RIVER MANNERS

Running a popular river like the Arkansas requires some knowledge of river etiquette:

- It's usually easier for a kayaker to yield the right-of-way than it is for a raft.

- Don't pull out from shore into a line of boats traveling together. Ask how many are still coming and wait until the last one passes.
- If another boat appears to be in trouble see if you can help. They might be missing an important piece of equipment.
- Use the 50-50 rule when traveling in a group of rafts. Don't get farther than 50 yards away from the boat ahead of you in case it has a problem, but don't get closer than 50 feet because of the danger of a pile-up.
- If you must pass another boat, ask first and do so only when there's plenty of room and enough time before the next narrow channel.
- When parking at put-in and take-out points be sure to leave enough room for buses and trailers to turn around.
- Inflate and deflate your boat away from congested areas.

CONSERVATION

Courtesy toward the river and the surrounding land must also be a consideration of every river traveler.

- Pack out what you take in. This includes garbage and solid human waste.
- Avoid stopping on grassy shores even though they may look inviting. These environments are especially sensitive to the pressure of boats and footsteps. Some have already been defoliated. Look instead for beaches of sand or gravel. Likewise don't set up a tent or lay your sleeping bag on a patch of grass or wildflowers.
- Throw nothing in the water—not even cigarette butts or

orange peels.

- Never build a new fire pit when one is already present nearby. Better yet, don't build a fire at all. Taking wood from the forest may prevent valuable trace minerals from returning to the soil. Camp stoves are more efficient for cooking anyway and they don't interfere with your view of the stars. If you must have a fire, collect only wood that has fallen to the ground. Dead branches and snags are used by wildlife for perches and homes.

LIVING AND CAMPING ON THE ARKANSAS

Arkansas Valley weather is typical of the southern Rockies during the summer: bright morning sunshine with a chance of afternoon thundershowers. The thunderstorms present two dangers. Lightning is one. It usually seeks the high points rather than the canyon bottoms. But in more open areas like Webster Park or the last miles of the Browns Canyon run, lightning can be a definite hazard.

Flash floods are the other hazard caused by thunderstorms. When camping or picnicking at the mouth of a side canyon, always be aware that even if the sky is clear where you are, a flash flood may be descending from a sudden cloudburst in the mountains, many miles away. Camp on fairly high, solid ground—not on the comfortable surface of a sandy wash. Also, don't forget to tie your boats individually to a stout tree or rock at night. For an example of a flash flood's power, turn to mile 61.8 in chapter 4.

Camping along the Arkansas is legal practically anywhere on land owned by the Bureau of Land Management (BLM). If you camp in a backcountry location where there are no facilities, bring a portable toilet. All you need is a large army surplus ammo box (also called a rocket box), some trash bags, something to use for a seat, and a bit of formaldehyde for the smell.

Late in the season the river water becomes very clear and looks clean enough to drink—don't. You never know what a cow might have done upstream. To kill parasites: boil the water, filter it properly or treat it chemically. Water in the sidestreams may be even more contaminated than that in the river.

THE RIVER AND THE LAW

Commercial users must obtain a permit from the BLM to use public land along the river for lunch stops, camping and even for scouting rapids. Outfitters new to the area should contact the BLM (appendix 1) for additional restrictions.

As of 1985, private boaters are not required to have a permit to run the Arkansas. However, Colorado law does require a type I, II, III or IV personal flotation device to be worn at all times by all boaters while on the river. This law is enforced with periodic spot checks. Other required equipment for commercial rafts includes a minimum of one spare life jacket for every three rafts, one bow or stern line (minimum 10 feet), one spare oar/paddle per raft, first–aid kit, repair kit, minimum throw bag, pump and bailing device. It is also suggested that a bucket, proper clothes to prevent hypothermia and matches be brought along.

Have a good trip, and remember, when in doubt, scout it out.

Paddle raft on the Arkansas River with views of Mount Ouray (left) and Chipeta (right), viewed from the 291 bridge (mile 42.8).

Part II

The River—Mile by Mile

3 RIVER TRIPS

If you're the operator of a raft, canoe or kayak on the Arkansas you should read chapter 2, "Boating on the Arkansas," before taking any of the following trips. In order to familiarize yourself in advance with a section of river you plan to travel, read all of the entries below which correspond to that trip before you leave the shore.

Most of those trips which are under 15 miles can be completed in well under a day. A full day should be allowed for trips in the 20- to 30-mile range.

The river access points listed are those which are most commonly used at the time of this writing. Driving directions are given. Additional put-in and take-out points will surely become available with increasing use.

Expert boaters may think some of the rapids described in this chapter have been overrated in terms of danger. However, the information was written mainly for novice and intermediate boaters.

PAN-ARK LODGE BRIDGE TO GRANITE: Mile 0 to Mile 6.4

The six-and-a-half mile section from the Pan-Ark Lodge Bridge to Granite is runnable for kayaks, but it may not be suitable for rafts. The water is relatively flat and shallow but surprisingly fast. It's a good place for advanced beginners to practice their skills.

Put In
Pan-Ark Lodge Bridge (mile 0). Just south of the Pan-Ark Lodge on Highway 24 (ten miles south of Leadville and twenty-one miles north of Buena Vista) turn east onto a dirt road to the bridge. CAUTION: put in below the bridge because it is too low to pass beneath at most levels.

Take Out
Granite Bridge (mile 6.4). In Granite turn east on Chaffee County Road 397.

Mile 0
Pan-Ark Lodge Bridge. River access. Do not float beneath.

Mile 4
Lake Creek Confluence. The class II rapid at this point is the only real rapid on this run.

Mile 6.4
Granite Bridge. River access.

GRANITE CANYON: Mile 6.4 to Mile 8.5
This short picturesque canyon is suitable for intermediate boaters but caution is required in a few spots. It may be run by experts as a warm-up for Pine Creek (class VI) which occurs just a few miles downstream.

Put In
   Granite Bridge. See take out for last trip.

Take Out
   Several rough dirt roads (mile 8.5) lead down to the river from Highway 24 in the vicinity of the old rock dam. Some of these are posted with no-trespassing signs. Remember, Pine Creek Rapid (class VI) is just downstream.

Mile 6.4
   Granite Bridge. River access.

Mile 7.3
   Maytag Rapid. Class III. Maytag occurs near the beginning of Granite Canyon. It may be scouted by turning off of Highway 24 just north of the "Mountain Transportation" historical sign. Maytag's gradient is steep but there are no serious holes. The fact that there are two rapids on the Arkansas called Maytag (mile 85.4) attests to the river's abundant whitewater. Some easy class II–III waves follow which require careful maneuvering in low water.

Mile 8.4
   Old Rock Dam. Class IV–VI. River access. Practically everyone portages here. The broken-down dam below the mouth of Granite Canyon may be seen from Highway 24. It can be run by those who don't mind bashing their boats on the rocks or risking getting hung up on a cable strung across the river.

Mile 8.5
  River access.

PINE CREEK CANYON:
Mile 8.5 to Mile 12.4

  Pine Creek is the most notorious rapid on the Arkansas and possibly in the state. Its treacherous upper part is attempted by expert kayakers only. Rafters generally leave it alone. Swimmers in Pine Creek risk serious injury because of the very fast water and numerous rocks. The rapid's difficulty directly varies with the water level. To scout from Highway 24, look for a high, steep slope of loose brownish rock immediately east of the river. Then pull out at the turnout on the east side of the road. A railroad access road leads down to the water.

Put In

  See put in and take out for last trip.

Take Out

  Scott's Bridge (mile 12.7). From Highway 24, ten miles north of Buena Vista and twenty-one miles south of Leadville, look for a pair of bridges over the river, one of which is severely broken down (it is hoped that this hazard will be removed by the time you read this). River access is available either on the east shore a few tenths of a mile above the bridge or below the bridge if you don't mind running Number One in Rapids One Through Six (see mile

l2.5). The landowners here have been very tolerant of river
users in the past, so please be respectful of their property.
Littering or building new fire rings will only make it hard for
other river users in the future.

Mile 8.9
   Boulder field. Class II–III.

Mile 10.3
   Pine Creek Rapid. Class V–VI. An anvil-shaped
rock on river right marks the head of the rapid. Dirt roads on
each side of the river make portaging easy. Serious holes
and drops occur throughout but the "S-bends" just below the
creek's mouth and about midway into the main rapid are the
most technical part. Some prefer to put in just below the S-
bends as the gradient downriver lessens and there are more
places to make rescues. But there's still a good deal of class
IV water before the river mellows.

Mile 12.4
   River access on east shore. Take out as soon as you see
Scott's Bridge if you don't want to run Rapid Number One.

Mile 12.5
   Rapid Number One. Class IV–V. See next trip.

Mile l2.7
   Scott's Bridge. River access.

THE NUMBERS, ONE THROUGH SIX:
Mile 12.4 to Mile 17.1

A run through the Numbers is both technically challenging and physically demanding. Sober, expert boaters should be able to handle it at low to medium-high levels. This section is for those who think they're good and want to prove it. But don't ever try it unless you're sure you're good. Fatalities have occurred here.

Those attempting the Numbers should scout thoroughly or follow someone who is already familiar with the run. Scouting is especially important for Numbers Two, Four and Five if you're a first timer, but nasty holes occur throughout. A dirt road paralleling the river to the west (but not always next to it) facilitates scouting and makes it possible to put in and take out at a number of places other than those described below.

Rafters using oars should keep their boats light because of the almost continual maneuvering even between rapids. At higher levels it's difficult to tell where one Number stops and the next one begins. Paddle rafts are seldom run here except by the most experienced crews.

This is the site of the annual Colorado Cup Kayaking Championship. In some years, the nationals are held here as well.

A gauge at Scott's Bridge (mile 12.7) is used by many boaters as their principle indicator of the Arkansas' volume. According to Fletcher Anderson in his book *Rivers of the Southwest*, three feet on the gauge means 1,200 cfs and six feet on the gauge corresponds to 3,500 cfs.

Put In
   Scott's Bridge. See take out for last trip.

Take Outs
   Chaffee County 371 Bridge (mile 14.1). Eight
miles north of Buena Vista turn east from Highway 24 at the
sign for the Otero Pump Station. Rapid Number Five is immediately after the bridge.
   The railroad bridge (mile 17.1) is an easy take out for
both rafters and kayakers. It can be found by turning east
from Highway 24 eight miles north of Buena Vista onto
Chaffee County 371 at the sign for the Otero Pump Station.
Cross the river above Rapid Number Five, take your first
right and drive south 3.2 miles.

Mile 12.4
   River access on east shore.

Mile 12.5
   Rapid Number One. Class IV–V. This boulder field
can be as treacherous as any of the other Numbers. It ends
at Scott's Bridge. Many people put in below Rapid Number
One for convenience.

Mile 12.7
   Scott's Bridge. River access. (Please don't litter).

Mile 12.9
   Number Two. Class IV–V. Watch out for big bad
hole in the center of the first drop.

Mile 13.2
  Number Three. Class III. Most of the rapid consists
of long standing waves with big troughs. The hole at the
bottom isn't runnable during low water.

Mile 13.4
  Number Four. Class IV–V. This is the longest of
the six and one of the toughest. Swimming Four often
means getting battered up by the rocks. A series of big holes
in the first half of the rapid is followed by a rock garden
where the river widens out and curves left. A number of
holes and waves give the section between Rapids Four and
Five a rating of class III–IV.

Mile 13.8
  Ender Rock. The large rock about midway between
Rapids Four and Five is an excellent play spot for kayakers
at most water levels.

Mile 14.1
  Chaffee County 371 Bridge. River access.

Mile 14.2
  Number Five. Class IV–V. Another toughy. Five
can be scouted in advance from the Chaffee County 371
Bridge during your shuttle. The bad hole right after the
bridge can be missed on the left. The four-foot drop after the
river bends right may be hit if done properly. But work your
way left immediately afterward or the river will push you
to the right and into the rocks.

Kayaker (Dan Hicks) doing an ender at Ender Rock (mile 13.8).

Mile 15.2

Number Six. Class IV–V. After picking your way through the rock garden be prepared to miss the two big holes on the left followed by two more big holes on the right.

Mile 15.8

Number Seven. Class IV–V. While not quite as serious as the "Big Six," the number seven designation given to this series of holes in the long straight section of the river below Rapid Six serves as a reminder that you can't let up yet.

Mile 17.1

Railroad Bridge. River access. The short section above the railroad bridge is fairly rocky but its gradient isn't as steep as that of the Numbers upstream. It could be considered class IV in high water but it is more often rated class III–III+. Remember, it's a long walk out from this part of the river.

Mile 18.3

Mount Harvard Estates Bridge. Private property. No river access.

FROG ROCK RUN (WILDHORSE CANYON): Mile 17.1 to Mile 26

This is one of the few extended sections of the Arkansas where the river mellows enough to let you enjoy the backcountry without being distracted by the commercial rafting hordes. Its a good run for intermediate boaters although at very high levels it should probably be left to the experts.

Put In
Railroad Bridge. See take out for previous trip. NOTE: The Mount Harvard Estates Bridge (mile 18.3) is private property and cannot be used as a put in or take out.

Take Outs
Fourmile Bridge (mile 21.9). Turn east at the stoplight on Main Street in Buena Vista and then left at Colorado Avenue. Continue north 1.7 miles. Use this take out if you don't want to run House Rock Rapid (mile 22.7). NOTE: The banks on the river's west side are steep and overgrown making access for kayakers difficult and for rafters impossible. The east side is private property.

Baseball Field (mile 23.6). Turn east at the Buena Vista stoplight and continue on Main Street all the way to the baseball field next to the river. The take out is near the concrete remnants of an old dam just below the USGS gauge. Access to this property may be limited in the future. For an update call the Buena Vista Town Clerk at 395-8643.

Johnson Village (mile 26). The River's Edge Motel near the southwest corner of the Highway 24/285 bridge in Johnson Village allows river access for private boaters on weekdays and after 11:00 A.M. on summer weekends. You must check with the office before putting in or taking out here. The banks immediately next to the bridge are public land, but they are very steep, affording access only for kayakers.

Mile 18.3
Mount Harvard Estates Bridge. Private property. No river access.

Mile 20.1
Frog Rock. Class III–IV. The graffiti-covered phallic monolith called Elephant Rock on County Road 371 east of the river is a good landmark for scouting. Elephant Rock is just up the road from the Fourmile Bridge (see take outs above). Frog Rock Rapid is found by walking north after reaching the river from Elephant Rock. This four-foot drop contains a cruncher hole and is best run on the left. Below 800 cfs rafts will have to be portaged.

Mile 20.5
Boulder Field. Class III. This 500-yard section shortly after Frog Rock Rapid is easy to read. It precedes one of the narrowest spots on the river—a notch through solid rock which is little more than 12 feet wide. Some additional class III water occurs within the next mile and a half.

Mile 21.8
Railroad Bridge.

Mile 21.9
Fourmile Bridge. River access.

Mile 22.7
House Rock Rapid. Class III–IV. Here the river splits around a large divider rock which can cause problems.

Beware of logjams. Scout on river left only. No trespassing warnings have been painted on the boulders on river right with obnoxious red paint. The right side is probably the best route through the rapid.

Mile 23.6
Buena Vista Baseball Field. River access. Look for the concrete abutments which mark the first of two old dam sites at Buena Vista.

Mile 24.9
Old Dam. Class II–III. The jagged, rocky barrier which remained after the old dam was dynamited once stretched from shore to shore, but a chute now allows for the safe passage of boats. A bit of lively class III water follows.

Mile 26
Johnson Village, Highway 24/285 Bridge. River access is just downstream from the bridge on river right.

THE MILKRUN: Mile 26 to Mile 29.6
This is a good section for intermediate boaters and advanced beginners. A small diversion dam about midway through the run is the only potential problem. The channel leading to the dam is on the left and is marked with a warning sign well in advance. Just below the Johnson Village put in there are some big safe class III waves during high water. During low water this is not a good run for rafts.

Put In

Johnson Village. See take out for last trip.

Take Out

Fisherman's Bridge (mile 29.6). From U.S. 285 turn east onto Chaffee County 30l, two miles north of Nathrop and 3.5 miles south of the junction of Highways 285 and 24. Cross the river on Fisherman's Bridge and turn right at the top of the hill.

Mile 26

Johnson Village. River access.

Mile 26.9

Railroad Bridge.

Mile 29.6

Fisherman's Bridge. Watch your heads when passing under the bridge during high water. The take out is about 100 yards downstream on river left. Look for the steps and the boat balancing railing leading up the bank.

BROWNS CANYON: Mile 29.6 to Mile 45.6

Browns Canyon is one of the country's most popular commercial runs. So if you're offended by long convoys of rafts, avoid the summer weekends. The canyon's fast, tight channels offer a challenging run for careful intermediate and advanced rafters and kayakers. There are a few nasty suckholes at higher levels. During very high water Browns should be run only by expert boaters who know the canyon or are following someone who does. Below approximately 600 cfs Browns Canyon is impassable for the average 14-foot raft.

Although most of the land on the west side of the two mile approach to Browns Canyon past Ruby Mountain is private, most in the canyon itself is owned by the Bureau of Land Management (BLM). The area east of the railroad is a proposed Federal Wilderness Area. Unlike the Arkansas Canyon downriver, there is no highway through Browns.

Put Ins

Fisherman's Bridge. See take out for last trip.

Ruby Mountain BLM Campground (mile 31.5). Cross the river as if going to the Fisherman's Bridge BLM river access point (see above) but continue straight and turn right on Chaffee County 300. Follow this for about two miles. Commercial users are not allowed river access here, but a few companies have leased the private land immediately next to the BLM campground for their own use.

Take Outs

Hecla Junction BLM Campground (mile 39.5). On the east side of Highway 285, look for County Road 194 and the Hecla Junction sign 7.4 miles south of Nathrop and 1.6 miles north of the Highway 291 junction. The two-mile dirt road to the river is passable to most two-wheel-drive vehicles but it can be slippery after a rain. When driving on this road keep to the right, watch out for buses and mind the speed limit.

The Staircase in Browns Canyon.

Highway 291 Bridge (mile 42.8). Six miles northwest of Salida. The bank here is too steep for rafters. Some of the land is private so it may be necessary to ask for permission.

Big Bend (mile 45.6). There are two river access points where the Arkansas makes a sweeping S curve at the north end of Adobe Park. The Big Bend area can be found by turning east on Chaffee County 165 from U.S. 285, four miles north of Poncha Springs. Approximately one tenth of a mile down County Road 165 a log fence and locked chain mark the River Runners Take Out for which there is a charge. Information can be obtained from River Runners Ltd. (719-539-2144). A tenth of a mile further down County Road 165 is a large open area where there is another take out. But this is open only to commercial rafting companies who are members of AROA (Appendix 1). CAUTION: There is not enough clearance to pass beneath the Chaffee County 191 Bridge at mile 42.5 when the river is running above about 4,500 cfs. Unfortunately, the land here is private and the owners will not allow portaging at the time of this writing.

Mile 29.7

Fisherman's Bridge. BLM boat access.

Mile 31.5

Ruby Mountain. BLM boat access and campground.

Mile 32.0

Footbridge. Owned by Browns Campground.

Mile 34.2
Railroad Bridge. After two to four miles (depending on your put in) of class I and II water, this bridge marks the beginning of Browns Canyon.

Mile 34.6
Canyon Doors. Class III–IV. Pull over on river left to scout Pinball before reaching this pair of ridges sloping down on either side of the river. The large high water waves which form in the narrow channel at Canyon Doors should be avoided so that you'll be in good shape to move right for Pinball.

Mile 34.7
Pinball Rapid. Class IV. This complex boulder field can have some unfriendly holes and rocks which require some very crisp boat handling to avoid. At the top of the rapid, right after the Canyon Doors, a hazardous pour-over forms in the center of the channel during high water. After missing the pour-over, more technical maneuvering is required to dodge the rocks and pass through an S turn on river right. Calm water follows before Zoom Flume.

Mile 35.5
Zoom Flume Rapid. Class III–IV. From upriver, the head of Zoom Flume resembles a waterfall's sudden drop–off. The sand beach with the large eddy on river left approximately 200 yards above this steep rapid is a good place to scout. The ride through Zoom is relatively safe albeit very fast and wet. In the short bit of calm water immediately after Zoom it's a good idea to eddy out and bail

so that your boat is light enough to maneuver through the upcoming boulder field.

Mile 35.7

Boulder Field below Zoom Flume. Class III. The best channel here is on the left. The dangerous high water pour-over which forms at the end of this quarter-mile section can be missed fairly easily. A quarter mile of easy water pre-cedes Big Drop.

Mile 36.6

Big Drop Rapid. Class III–IV. Good taste prevents printing Big Drop's other name. To scout, pull over near the end of the calm stretch which occurs just before the river narrows and picks up speed. Hitting the meat of Big Drop's main wave is fairly safe but the two high water reflective waves coming off the left bank have flipped more than one raft. When in doubt, stay right. Also, watch out for the boat-wrapping rock at the end of the fast water after the river bends back to the left. A short, calm stretch precedes the Staircase.

Mile 36.9

The Staircase (The Seven Stairs). Class III. One of the nicest things about this series of drop-offs followed by easy standing waves is that it lasts awhile. During high water there are so many waves it's impossible to differentiate one stair from another. It begins where the river narrows and the canyon walls become very steep. The first two stairs are little more than riffles but the third through the seventh are quite lively. The big rock which appears in the middle of the fifth stair during low water can be missed easily on river left, but it isn't visible until the last minute. At around 6,000 cfs a dangerous cresting wave forms in the seventh stair.

Mile 37.6

Widowmaker Rapid. Class IV–V. To scout, eddy out immediately after the Staircase on river left. Widowmaker's most notorious part is the Toilet Bowl where the river is directed into a whirlpool-like current by a large rock on river left. In very high water this rock forms a dangerous keeper-type suckhole which can be easily avoided on the right. Following the Toilet Bowl in consecutive downstream order are: a large divider rock, a bad high-water hole on river right, pointed rocks on river left exposed during low water and the large "House Rock" blocking most of the channel on river right. Watch out for logjams here. There follows some easily missed high-water suckholes around the bend, a bit of class II water and a long flat stretch before Raft Ripper.

Mile 38

Jump Rock. The steep bank which must be climbed to reach this popular lunch spot is extremely hazardous because of the loose rocks. Bones have been broken here.

Mile 38.5

Raft Ripper (Snake Slide). Class III–IV. The alternate name for Raft Ripper suggests the way most of the river slides down from right to left and the way a raft must snake

between two ominously pointed rocks which are exposed at
lower water levels. Above 5000 cfs a large cresting wave
capable of stalling and flipping large rafts forms on river left
at the end of the main current coming out of Raft Ripper.

Mile 38.7

The Graveyard (Boulder field below Raft Ripper).
Class III. This section is largely covered during high water.
Rafting The Graveyard during low water can be an exciting
technical experience. A quarter mile past the boulder field
a short series of class II-III standing waves precede the calm
water leading to Hecla Junction.

Mile 39.1

Hecla Junction BLM Campground and River Access.
After the sand beach at Hecla Junction (river right), some
riffles and easy waves precede the long, calm stretch leading to Seidel's.

Mile 40.5

Seidel's Suckhole. Class IV–V. It's been said that the
river gods live at the bottom of Seidel's. Worse suckholes
exist but few are as hard to miss. Although more boats flip
here than anyplace else on the entire river, the calm (but
fast) water which follows makes swimming to the right
shore relatively easy. Still, it's a good idea to station a
rescue boat and at least one person with a throwline below
the rapid because Twin Falls and a small boulder field lie a
short distance downstream. To scout, follow the well-worn
path that begins on the right shore just before the river

funnels into the fast channel above the rapid. Seidel's lies about a quarter mile downstream at the point where the Arkansas' width is abruptly cut in half before dropping over a steep ledge. For a class V rapid, Seidel's is short. Timing, positioning and power are the keys to a successful run. Some go right down the tongue and blast through the main hole. A more conservative strategy is to push through the right reflective wave in an attempt to reach the smooth chute to the right of the hole. Skirting the hole on the left may also be possible at certain levels. Don't let your bow get caught in the backwater from the pour-overs on each side of the river at the top of the main tongue or you may get turned sideways. Bail thoroughly after Seidel's because

Disheveled rafters, after running Seidel's Suckhole (mile 40.5).

you'll want a light boat to avoid the boulders after Twin Falls.

Mile 40.7

Twin Falls (Lower Seidel's). Class III. This straight shot down the center lies within sight of Seidel's. During very low water, be careful in an oar raft not to crunch the passengers in the back. The boulder field after Twin Falls can be missed with a hard drive to the right.

Mile 42.5

Stone Bridge, Chaffee County Road 191. This concrete bridge appears soon after the end of Browns Canyon. At levels above 4,500 cfs there isn't enough room to float beneath it. But be aware that because of the ill will of the landowners you'll be breaking the law if you portage to save your life. Taking out at Stone Bridge will also make you a trespasser. A good eddy for two or three rafts exists very close to the bridge upstream on river right.

Mile 42.8

Highway 291 Bridge. Possible river access.

Mile 45

Squaw Creek Rapid. Class II–III. This rapid occurs on a blind left curve less than a mile above Adobe Park. Although it isn't very difficult, it is necessary to get into position before you see the rapid. When the highway becomes visible you're getting close. For the best ride, move to the left before the river bends left.

Mile 45.6

Big Bend (Adobe Park). The River Runners Take Out is in a grove of large cottonwoods immediately after the goat farm on river right. This area is also used by River Runners as a campground. The current here can be swift but an artificial rock jetty provides a good eddy. The AROA take out is just downstream.

POSSIBLE DANGER: A low-head dam exists less than four miles down river. (See next trip).

THE SALIDA RUN: Mile 45.6 to Mile 54.3

The gentle water along this picturesque section would make it suitable for beginning boaters were it not for the single most life-threatening spot on the river—a six-foot low-head dam which creates a severe, boat-holding waterfall across the entire channel. At the time of this writing, plans are underway to construct a chute in the dam for the safe passage of rafters, kayakers and canoeists. For an update, call one of the rafting companies listed in appendix 2.

Put Ins

Adobe Park or the Highway 291 Bridge. See take outs for last trip.

Take Outs

Colorado Division of Wildlife land (mile 50.4). From Highway 29l, a short distance west of Salida, turn north at the sign for Spiral Drive onto Chaffee County l75. Then turn left onto the dirt road that parallels the west side of the river to a turnaround in a grove of cottonwoods about a half mile up.

FIBArk Building/Riverside Park, Salida (mile 51.7). These two river access points occur on the east shore, upstream and downstream respectively of the F Street Bridge in Salida.

Salida East BLM Recreation Site (mile 54.3). One and a half miles east of Salida on Highway 50 and immediately after the Four Seasons Mobile Home Park look for either of two unmarked dirt roads leading down to the river. One of the dirt roads begins between the two guardrails and the other begins after the second guardrail.

Mile 48.1

Chaffee County l66 Bridge.

Mile 49.3

Smeltertown Dam. DANGER: DO NOT RUN THE DAM. A sign on river left advises that you take out immediately. The landowners on the left side of the dam allow portaging at your own risk. (See the introduction to this section of the river.)

Mile 50.4

Colorado Division of Wildlife land. River access and camping.

Mile 50.6

Highway 291 Bridge. This is the second time the river passes beneath Highway 291. The first was at mile 42.8.

Mile 50.8

Chaffee County 175 Bridge. Watch your heads during high water.

Mile 51.8

FIBArk Building, F Street Bridge, Riverside Park. River access. The gates for the slalom event held during Salida's annual FIBArk celebration are placed above and below the bridge in mid-June.

Mile 53.9

Stockyards Bridge.

Mile 54.3

Salida East BLM boat access and camping.

THE UPPER ARKANSAS CANYON: Mile 54.3 to Mile 74.5

Before the rise in popularity of Browns Canyon, the Arkansas River between Salida and Cotopaxi accounted for a greater percentage of boating traffic than it does today. The upper half of the great Arkansas Canyon is still the course for the annual 26-mile downriver race held each June during FIBArk. (See mile 5l in chapter 4.)

Seasoned river travelers are sometimes put off by the fact that Highway 50 hugs much of the river's southern shore from Salida all the way to Parkdale. Also, the Upper Arkansas Canyon is characterized by several stretches of flat water and, with a few exceptions, mellower rapids than those in other parts of the river (making it a good place for less experienced boaters to develop their skills). But the Upper Arkansas Canyon contains the most fascinating geology on the river and the rural beauty of Pleasant Valley backed by the majestic Sangre de Cristo Mountains is unmatched.

Put Ins

See take outs for last trip.

Swissvale Manor (mile 59.5) on the north side of Highway 50 may also be used for river access but ask the owners.

Take Out

Vallie Bridge, Fremont County 45 (mile 69.8). The left shoreline two hundred yards above the bridge has been used as a put in and take out but the owners would prefer that it not be regarded as a public river access point.

Canyon Liquors (mile 74.5). The store and camp-ground are one mile east of the center of Cotopaxi on U.S. 50. There is a nominal charge for river access.

Mile 54.3

Salida East. BLM river access and camping.

Mile 55.1

Bear Creek Rapids. Class III-IV. This long section is in two parts beginning at the Bear Creek confluence. The most serious spot is a large but easily missed reflective wave which forms off the left bank during high water immediately after a straight and narrow 50-yard channel near the end of the rapids.

Several moderate class II+ to III- rapids occur between Bear Creek and Badger Creek which have been called, in downstream order: Bed Creek, Barrel and Slanting Rock Rapids.

Mile 57

Footbridge.

Mile 57.7

Wellsville Bridge.

Mile 58.6

Spider Rapids. Class II–III. Named for a spider-like chunk of concrete studded with reinforcement bar on river right, this rapid occurs where the river bends to the right at the base of a steep earthen cliff on river left. Large standing waves form on the rapid's left side during high water.

Mile 59.5

Swissvale Manor. River access and commercial camping.

Mile 61.2

Rincon BLM Recreation Site. River access.

Mile 61.8

Badger Creek Rapid. Class III–IV. At one time there was hardly even a rapid here. Then in 1978 a flash flood out of Badger Creek carried a huge rock into the center of the main channel (see mile 61.8 in chapter 4). A long stretch of flat water is the signal that you're getting close. To scout, hug the left bank as soon as you see the black, trestle-type railroad bridge across Badger Creek on river left. Then pull into the creek as soon as possible. The Flume (mile 62) is a short distance downriver and can also be scouted at this time. During high water an easily missed, semi-keeper suck hole forms behind the big rock in Badger. During low water, passing the rock at close range can't be avoided and boats sometimes wrap, often because of indecision about which way to go. Many pass the rock on the left and quickly pull into the eddy behind it in order to avoid a ledge on the left shore which receives most of the current. It's also possible to pass the rock on the right, but watch out for logs on the right shore and be prepared to hit some smaller rocks in the narrow channel. Badger Creek Rapid changes more often than most rapids so this is a definite scout even if you've done it before.

Mile 62

The Flume (Locomotive, White Horse). Class III–IV. It's not uncommon for a rafter to relax after a successful run through Badger Creek Rapid and then flip in the Flume. This rapid can be scouted before or immediately after running Badger. An unfriendly suckhole sometimes forms at the ledge on river right. This is followed immediately by an overhanging rock face. Enter the rapid on the left and maintain a continuous effort to stay left against the current's rightward pull.

Mile 64
Fremont County 4 Bridge, Howard.

Mile 66
Fremont County 47 Bridge, Howard.

Mile 67.1
Tincup Rapid. Class III. This narrow chute isn't as bad as it looks from above. Enter slightly left of center. The sand beach on river right immediately after the rapid is a popular lunch spot but it's easy to miss during high water.

Mile 68
Red Rocks Rapid. Class II–III. In low water, the best route starts out on the right and then passes through a narrow channel to the left.

Mile 69.8
Vallie Bridge, Fremont County 45.

Mile 71
Rock Garden (Railroad Rapid). Class III–IV. This boulder field pops up suddenly on a bend in the river. Work your way to the right between the rocks.

Mile 72.1

Fremont County 6 Bridge, Coaldale. There are actually two bridges here.

Mile 73.1

Cottonwood Rapid. Class III–IV. Soon after the river crosses the Pleasant Valley Fault Line (chapter 4, mile 73), it funnels between steep granitic cliffs and into Cottonwood Rapid. This is one of the most enjoyable bits of white-water on the entire river and the perfect finale to an all-day trip through the Upper Arkansas Canyon. Cottonwood's big standing waves are relatively safe. Enter slightly right of center for a straight shot down the middle. Some class II water and boulder dodging precedes Little Cottonwood.

Mile 73.5

Little Cottonwood Rapid. Class III. This short rapid is made up principally of what local guides call "the Black-hole." A hapless fisherman drowned here some years ago after falling into the river. The hole occurs on the far left side of the river and should be missed. Although the channel narrows, it does allow room for the safe passage of a raft.

Mile 74.5

Canyon Liquors. A sign advertising refreshments on river right indicates that this river access point and camp-ground is coming up.

THE LOWER ARKANSAS CANYON:
Mile 74.5 to Mile 96.8

As in the Upper Canyon, the river shares the Lower Arkansas Canyon with Highway 50. From the Canyon Liquor Store in Cotopaxi (mile 74.5) to the Texas Creek Bridge (mile 83.7) the river is fairly mellow with no rapids above class II. This would make a perfect run for advanced beginners and intermediates if the owner of the Texas Creek Store permitted river access on his land on river right just upstream from the bridge. This is the only logical take out for such a run. River access is possible at the Lone Pine BLM area (mile 77.8), but this would make for a very short trip if you started at Cotopaxi.

Immediately past the Texas Creek Bridge the river is much more spirited. During high water it's best left to the experts. During low water the section from Texas Creek to Pinnacle Rock is not a good run for rafts because of the many rocks in Three Forks Rapid (mile 88.2). From Pinnacle Rock to Parkdale the whitewater is superb and this stretch is still passable even when the water is too low to get through Browns Canyon. This part of the river is heavily used by commercial rafts causing crowding at the access points and potential traffic hazards.

Put Ins

See put ins and take outs for last trip.

Cotopaxi (mile 76). The left shore is private. The right shore below the bridge can be used for river access, but the water here is very fast above 1000 cfs and the traffic on Highway 50 can be a problem.

There are a few turnouts below the Loma Linda KOA Campground on Highway 50 (mile 77.4) a mile and a half east of Cotopaxi which can be used for river access.

Pinnacle Rock (mile 89.1). Five and a half miles east of Texas Creek and ten miles west of the Parkdale Bridge, the thin, tower-like, flat-topped rock standing between the highway and the river will be obvious.

Lone Pine (mile 89.3). A few tenths of a mile east of Pinnacle Rock (not to be confused with Lone Pine BLM area at mile 77.8.)

Salt Lick BLM boat access (mile 90.7). Nine and a half miles west of the Parkdale Bridge and seven miles east of Texas Creek. Put in here if you want to avoid Three Rocks Rapid (class IV–V) at mile 90.3.

Take Out

Parkdale BLM Boat Access (mile 96.8). Two miles west of the Parkdale Bridge and thirteen miles east of Texas Creek. WATCH THE TRAFFIC.

Mile 74.5

Canyon Liquors. River access and camping. There is a charge. Check at the store.

Mile 76

Cotopaxi Bridge and Rapid. Class II. Some fun waves occur beneath the bridge. CAUTION: during high water make sure in advance that there's enough clearance to get under the bridge. River access may be possible downstream from the bridge on river right.

Mile 77.0
KOA Rapid. Class II. Turnouts below the Loma Linda KOA campground may be used for river access.

Mile 77.8
Lone Pine BLM river access. Take out here if you don't want to run Texas Creek Rapid (class III–III+) at mile 83.7. The river access point referred to as Lone Pine by the local guides is actually at mile 89.3.

Mile 78.9
Warm up Rapid. Class II.

Mile 79.7
Gosh Awful Rapid. Class II.

Mile 80.4
Snake Bridge. The cable strung across the river near the rock shop at Sand Gulch gets its name from the dead snake that used to hang from it. The cable may have been removed by the time you read this.

Mile 81.5
Footbridge. Owned by Arkansas Adventures Recreation Ranch.

Mile 83.7
Texas Creek Rapid and Bridge. Class III–III+. The rapid consists of some large waves on a fairly steep gradient immediately after the bridge. Enter on the left.

Mile 85.4

   Maytag Rapid. Class III–IV. The large waves here hit your boat from different directions as if you were in a washing machine. The best channel is on the far left, and in low water this is the only channel. Be careful you don't get washed into the rocks on the left shore. NOTE: in Granite Canyon there is another rapid called Maytag (mile 7.3).

Mile 85.9

   Maytag BLM Recreation Site and River Access. At the time of this writing, there is no sign marking this site from the road.

Mile 88.2

   Three Forks Rapid (Devil's Hole). Class III–IV. This long, lively rapid starts where the river splits into three channels just below the mouth of Echo Canyon. It can be run far left in high water but only the right channel is passable during low water. Watch out for concrete reinforcement bar along the right shore when the water is low. Below 500 cfs this rapid is unrunnable for rafts and a put in farther downstream should be used.

Mile 88.7

   Lose Your Lunch Rapid. Class III. A series of easy standing waves.

Mile 89.1

   Pinnacle Rock BLM River Access (Turkey Rock, Eagle Rock, Fred Rock). Look for the flat-topped rock projecting upward at an angle on river right.

Mile 89.3

Lone Pine River Access. **Named** for the lone ponderosa pine next to the river, this popular put in is often overcrowded. (Don't confuse this with the Lone Pine BLM area at mile 77.8)

Mile 90

Wakeup Rapid (Prelude). Class III. Another series of easy standing waves. This is a signal that Three Rocks is getting close.

Mile 90.3

Three Rocks Rapid (Reefer Madness). Class IV–V. Considered one of the most technical spots on the Arkansas, Three Rocks is generally portaged during high water. The name comes from the three large boulders in the middle of the rapid. For portaging or scouting: Pull into the left eddy at the end of a short calm stretch immediately after Wakeup Rapid and before the river bends to the right. A cottonwood and a large Ponderosa Pine will be visible downriver. This is a fairly small eddy so if you're in a raft don't take too long. (Courteous river travelers pull their boats all the way up on the bank while scouting to make room for others.) The worst part of Three Rocks is the hole which forms behind the middle rock. Missing it requires good technique but it's not difficult once you've mastered the formula: After rounding the bend above the rapid, stay in the center to avoid the small hole on the left and the large hole on the right. A reflective wave from the left side may then be surfed to the right as an aid in getting to the channel between the middle and right rock. A big cruncher hole at the bottom of the rapid can be missed with an immediate drive to the left after passing the three rocks.

Mile 90.7
Salt Lick BLM River Access.

Mile 91
Five Points Rapid. Class III–IV. The big hole just left of center at the bottom of this steep grade has flipped a boat or two. The BLM does not allow river access at their recreation site adjacent to the rapid. Some class II water follows.

Mile 92.4
Floodplain BLM area. This area is closed to vehicles at the time of this writing.

Mile 92.6
Spike Buck BLM River Access.

Mile 93.4
Spike Buck Rapid. Class IV. A straight stretch of flat water precedes this long exciting rapid. A series of holes down the rapid's center requires caution. It may be wise to just catch a piece of the upper holes so you'll be in good shape to move right and miss the very nasty hole at the bottom of the rapid.

Mile 94.7

Shark's Tooth Rapid (Grail's Falls, The Tube). Class III–IV. The river narrows down considerably here and runs directly next to the highway. Shark's Tooth is very lively but rarely causes any problems.

Mile 95.3

Double Dip Rapid. Class III-IV. The first of this rapid's two dips isn't present at certain water levels. The larger second dip (hole) should be missed to the right, but be careful not to get pushed into the shore.

Mile 95.9

Puppy Rapid and Puppy's Tail. Class III–IV. Puppy is little more than easy standing waves but the strong hydraulic about 200 yards downstream in Puppy's Tail (sometimes called Kamikaze) can flip boats during high water. It's best to sneak it to the right. During low water Puppy's Tail is just rocks.

Mile 96.8

Parkdale BLM River Access. Boats must be carried up and down the steep stairway. This is the last public take out before the Royal Gorge. CAUTION: be careful of the fast-moving traffic on Highway 50.

THE ROYAL GORGE:
Mile 96.8 to Mile l08.2

The Royal Gorge is one of the most scenically spectacular river trips in the country. The whitewater is also first-rate and, while it may not be quite as technical as Browns Canyon, the big hydraulics and fast current make the risks greater. This run should be completed only by experts. Intermediates should portage the more difficult rapids. The limits for safe rafting in the Gorge lie between about one and three thousand cfs. But the limits are sometimes pushed.

As with any expert run, the Gorge should be thoroughly scouted if it's your first time through and, if possible, done with somebody who's already familiar with it.

As in other parts of the river, scouting from river left is generally easiest because of the railbed. But the danger of being suddenly confronted by a fast freight or one of the quiet little electric work cars is especially pronounced in the Gorge because of the frequent whitewater noise and many sharp bends. Understandably, the railroad does not appreciate trespassing. If you scout from river right, try not to walk on the old metal water pipe. It may not support your weight.

At the time of this writing, the Gorge hasn't been choked with commercial rafts the way that Browns Canyon and the Lower Arkansas Canyon have. But it may just be a matter of time. Large numbers of boats in the Gorge could present a serious situation because of the small and infrequent eddies and fewer options to bypass holes.

NOTE: Do not eat lunch at the top of Sunshine Rapid. The small eddies on river right can't hold many rafts and practically everyone stops here to scout.

Put In

A run through the Gorge is often preceded with a run through the Arkansas Canyon beginning at the Lone Pine put in (mile 89.3). Those wanting to run just the Gorge should put in at the Parkdale BLM River Access Point (mile 96.8) two miles west of the Parkdale Bridge on Highway 50.

Take Out

Public Take Out (mile 107.1). After crossing the First Street Bridge from Highway 50 in Canon City, take your first right onto a paved road which soon turns to dirt. Drive north approximately .9 mile to a line of cottonwoods along the river. River access is available at a grassy area in the cottonwoods.

Centennial Park (mile 108.2). To use this take out, a dangerous low-head dam must be dealt with (mile 107.3). To find the park: Turn south on Fourth Street, cross the railroad and the river, and take the first right (Griffin Avenue).

Mile 96.8

Parkdale BLM River Access. Boats must be carried up and down the steep stairway. This is the last public river access before the Royal Gorge. CAUTION: be careful of the fast-moving traffic on Highway 50.

Mile 97.3

The Silver Bridge.

Mile 99
Parkdale Bridge. Highway 50.

Mile 99.7
Copper Gulch. If you stop to eat lunch at the large sandy wash on river right at Copper Gulch just above El Primero Rapid, please pull your kayak out of the water or float your raft to the downstream end of the beach to make room for others.

Mile 99.8
El Primero (On Your Mark, Guardian). Class III. The fun waves in El Primero begin about 100 yards past the small rock fortifications which were built on river left during the Railroad Wars.

Mile 100.1
El Segundo (Get Set). Class III. Although this rapid isn't difficult, some of the waves come at odd angles.

Mile 100.3
River's Edge. Class III. More fairly easy but very lively water.

Mile 100.5
Diversion Dam Rapid. Class III–IV. Just after the old dam site, enter this rapid on the right to miss a hole in the middle which contains concrete chunks with rebar. Then move left of another hole and back to the center between two big holes at the bottom.

Mile 100.6

Hollywood Hole. Class III–IV. If you plan to scout Sunshine Rapid it's probably best to miss this hole so that you can pull over on river right just past the foot bridge.

Mile 100.7

Foot Bridge. If this is used, only one person should cross at a time.

Mile.100.8

Sunshine Rapid (Caretaker). Class V. When a boat flips in the Gorge this is usually the place. It lies just below the narrow footbridge and the old white building on river right which was once used by the Canon City Waterworks Caretaker (don't confuse this structure with the one just upstream at the former dam site). Remember that the railroad does not appreciate trespassing so Sunshine should be scouted on river right. However, the best place to position people with throwbags is on river left. When scouting, be sure to walk all the way to the rapid's end to check out the worst spot—a bad suckhole in the center of the channel. This can be missed on the narrow chute to its left—but not too far left because of the large rock which forms a nasty pour-over at medium- to high-water levels. A few feet in either direction can make a big difference between success and failure. Most rafters run the entire rapid up to the chute on the far left, but low water may require some zigzagging. You may want to scout Sledgehammer concurrently with Sunshine.

Mile 101

 Sledgehammer Rapid. Class IV–V. A variety of successful lines have been taken through Sledgehammer but they all lead to the left of Clark's Hole. The rapid's head is marked by a huge boulder on river right. Immediately, you're confronted by Bird Drop Hole in the center of the river. About two-thirds of the way down the rapid, the current is funnelled into the river's most strangely shaped wave, appropriately named Envelope. Clark's Hole at the end of the rapid isn't very wide. But the way the current boils against the vertical face of a large boulder on river right is quite unappealing. The hole a few feet upriver

Raft emerging from Sunshine Rapid (mile 100.8).

should be run to the right to insure missing Clark's. A large unnamed hole in the center of the river beneath the footbridge just downstream from Sledgehammer can be challenging.

Mile 102.1

Dire Straits (The Narrows, Squeeze Box). Class III–IV. The most striking part of the Gorge begins just below a white cement chute built to carry a creek over the railroad track. At this point the river narrows into a series of large waves. Watch out for jagged rocks here in low water and the boat-ripping metal on the left wall.

Mile 102.6

The Fishbowl (Hanging Bridge and Royal Gorge Bridge). A flat bit of calm water at this historic location makes a good place to pause for a breather. The enthusiastic attention of the tourists who have come down on the Cog Railway may cause a river traveler to feel like some strange fish being watched in a fishbowl. Wall Slammer is scouted from the left.

Mile 102.7

Wall Slammer (Lewis' Wall, Bridge Rapid, The Wall). Class IV. Missing the steep cliff face on river right is compounded by the rocks on the left, one of which protrudes ominously during low water.

Mile 103.2

After The Bridge. Class IV–V. When the river is running above 2,000 cfs the big waves here come in quick succession making it hard to see what's coming up next. If there's any doubt about hitting something—miss it. Swimming here could be a long, cold and hazardous ordeal. It's best to stay slightly to the right because there's a very bad hydraulic on the left known as Boat Eater Hole which doesn't appear until you're atop the preceding wave. Because of its size and power, Boat Eater is also known as Greyhound Bus Hole. It occurs near the spot where the north canyon wall was blackened by smoke from the old steam locomotives. Other names for the big holes after the bridge include Corner Pocket and Corkscrew.

Mile 103.5

Soda Fountain Rock (Question Mark). Class IV. A large rock suddenly appears in center channel making it hard to decide which way to go. Go right, but move back to the left immediately after passing the rock in order to miss the nasty right shore.

Mile 103.8

Lion's Head. Class III–IV. Go right of this old, concrete bridge abutment where rebar may lurk beneath the waves.

Mile 103.9

Exit. Class III–IV. Right after Lion's Head some big fun waves end in a hole in the center of the river.

Mile 104.4

Water Pipe. Class III. Stay left as you pass beneath the water pipe. There's still plenty of class II and III water before the Gorge ends.

Mile 107.1

Public Take Out. The beach on river right in front of the big pink house is open to AROA members only. The public take out a quarter mile downstream on the same side of the river is hard to pick out from among the cottonwoods until you're very close. The adobe house across the river is a good landmark.

Mile l07.3

Low-head Dam. This dangerous waterfall has been run on the far left where the river forms a narrow chute, but beware of the deadly keeper hole which stretches across the rest of the river. Portaging or lining through is possible and recommended on the right shore.

Mile 108

First Street Bridge, Canon City.

Mile l08.2

Centennial Park, Canon City. River Access. This is preceded by a bit of class II water.

Kayaker taking a face shot.

CANON CITY TO FLORENCE:
Mile l08.2 to Mile 116.2

When the Arkansas leaves the mountains and flows out onto the plains it also leaves behind its serious whitewater. But hazards still exist. Between Canon City and Florence a number of downed trees block the channel making navigation both difficult and dangerous. Also, the Minnequa Dam must be portaged. No put-in and take-out points are listed here in order to discourage boating on this dangerous section.

Mile 108.3
Fourth Street Bridge, Canon City.

Mile 108.8
> *Ninth Street Bridge, Canon City, Highway 115.*

Mile 110.3
> *Raynolds Road Bridge.*

Mile 112.1
> *Fourmile Road Bridge.*

Mile 112.9
> *Railroad Bridge.*

Mile 113.4
> *Minnequa Dam.* Portage on river right.

Mile 116.2
> *Highway 67 Bridge, Florence.*

SWALLOWS CANYON:
Mile 116.2 to Mile l4l

If you enjoy calm water, canoeing this section is for you. While it isn't exactly a simple float trip, it isn't very technical either so long as you've had some experience on moving water. When the river is running high and fast, some extra caution is required. During low water, gravel bars and islands divide the river into two or three channels in many places. Beware of snags at all water levels. Swallows Canyon itself, which begins near mile 123, is both the safest and most scenic part of this section. If you take out on Pueblo Reservoir, remember that the wind on this manmade lake can be very severe.

Put In

Highway 67 Bridge (mile 116.2). From Highway 50 turn south on Highway 67 toward Florence.

Highway 115 Bridge (mile 118.8). From Highway 50 turn south on Highway 115. A dirt road leads down to the river at the southwest side of the bridge.

Take Out

The beginning of the Pueblo Reservoir (mile 140). Thirteen miles west of I-25, turn north off of Route 96 at the sign for the Pueblo Reservoir. After a half mile, turn left at the sign for the state wildlife area. This will put you on a good dirt and gravel road to the river (watch out for flash floods in the washes). Instead of turning at the wildlife area sign you may continue straight to the reservoir which ends at a concrete ramp leading into the water.

Mile 116.2

Highway 67 Bridge, Florence.

Mile 118.8

Highway 115 Bridge.

Mile 122.8

Railroad Bridge and Highway 120 Bridge, Portland. Swallows Canyon begins just downstream.

Mile 140

The beginning of Pueblo Reservoir. River Access.

Legend

Arkansas

Tributaries

Major Hwys.

Secondary
Roads

Railroads

Bridges

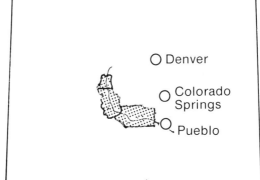

○ Denver

○ Colorado
Springs

○ Pueblo

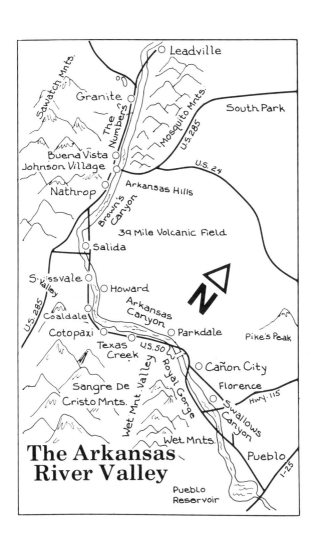

The Arkansas
River Valley

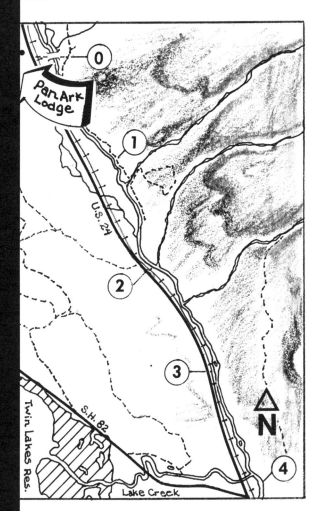

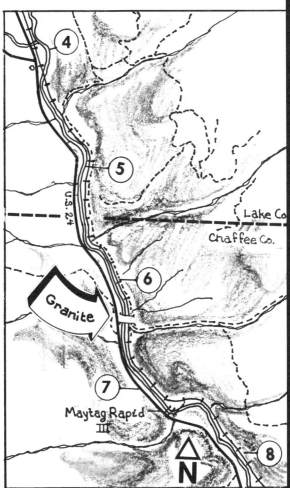

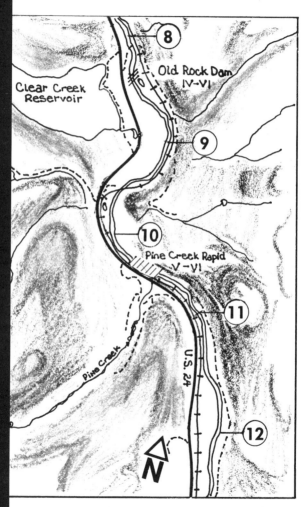

Old Rock Dam
IV–VI

Clear Creek
Reservoir

Pine Creek Rapid
V–VI

Pine Creek

U.S. 24

N

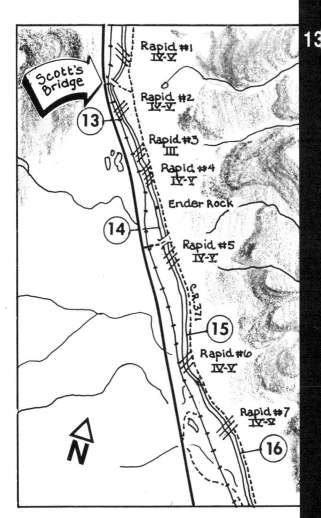

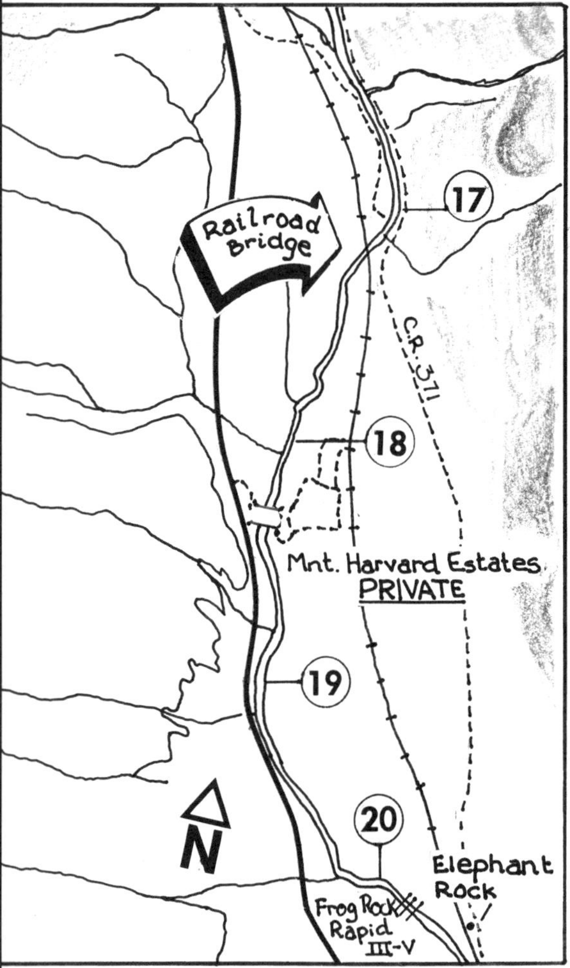

17

Railroad Bridge

17

C.R. 371

18

Mnt. Harvard Estates
PRIVATE

19

N

20

Elephant Rock

Frog Rock Rapid
III-V

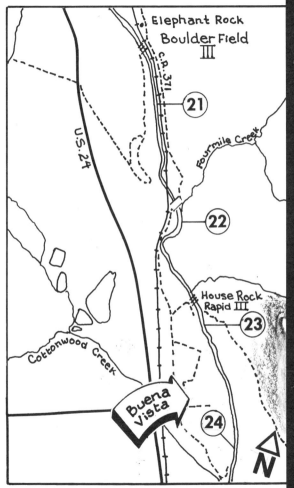

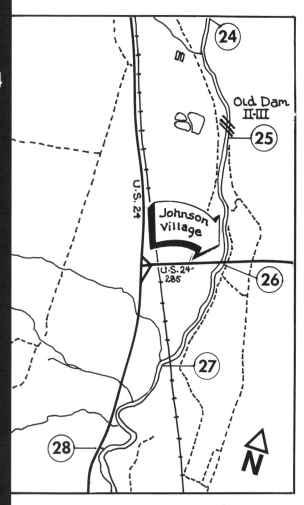

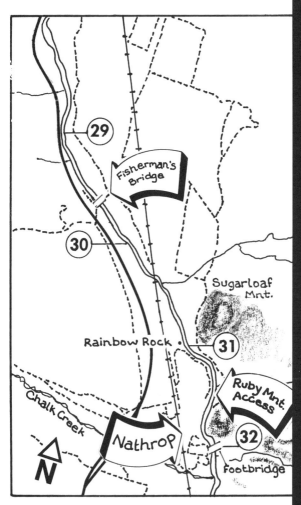

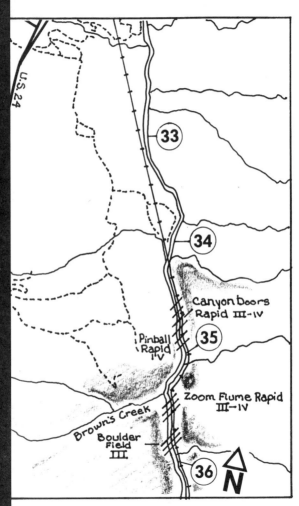

21

33

U.S. 24

33

34

Canyon Doors
Rapid III–IV

Pinball
Rapid
IV

35

Zoom Flume Rapid
III–IV

Brown's Creek

Boulder
Field
III

36

N

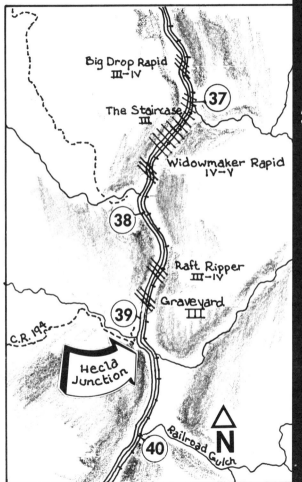

Big Drop Rapid
III–IV

37

The Staircase
III

Widowmaker Rapid
IV–V

38

Raft Ripper
III–IV

Graveyard
III

39

C.R. 194

Hecla
Junction

Railroad Gulch

40

N

37

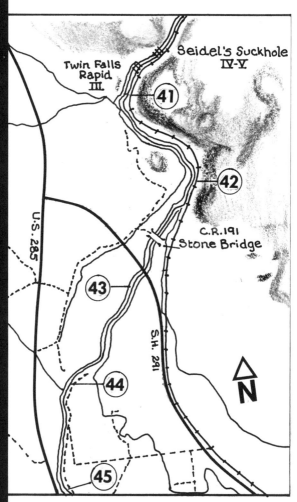

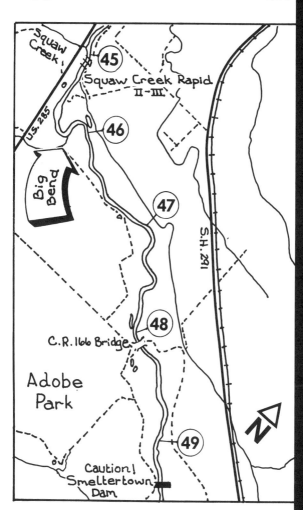

Squaw Creek

(45)

Squaw Creek Rapid
II-III

U.S. 285

(46)

Big
Bend

(47)

S.H. 291

(48)

C.R. 166 Bridge

Adobe
Park

N

(49)

Caution!
Smeltertown
Dam

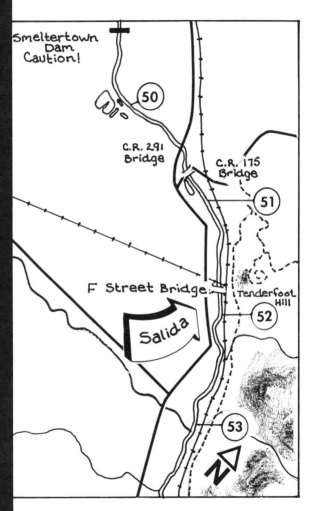

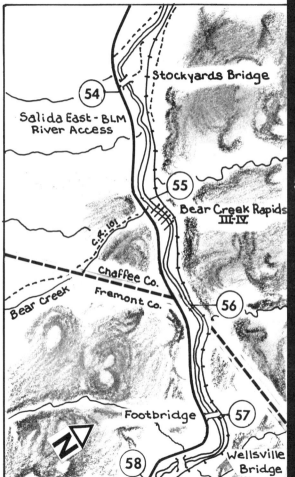

Stockyards Bridge

54

Salida East - BLM
River Access

55

Bear Creek Rapids
III-IV

C.R. 101

Chaffee Co.

Bear Creek

Fremont Co.

56

Footbridge

57

Wellsville
Bridge

58

54

58

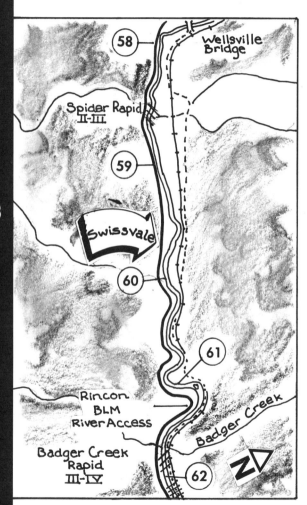

58

Wellsville Bridge

Spider Rapid
II-III

59

Swissvale

60

61

Rincon
BLM
River Access

Badger Creek

Badger Creek
Rapid
III-IV

62

N

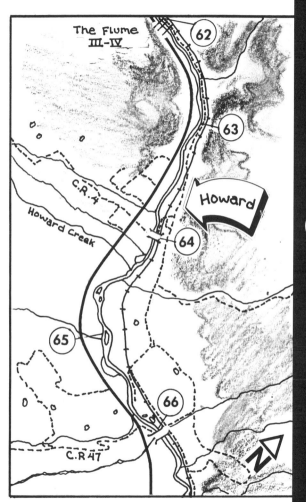

The Flume
III–IV

62

63

C.R. 4

Howard Creek

Howard

64

65

66

C.R 47

N

62

67

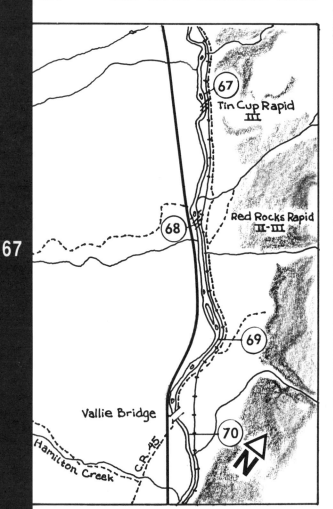

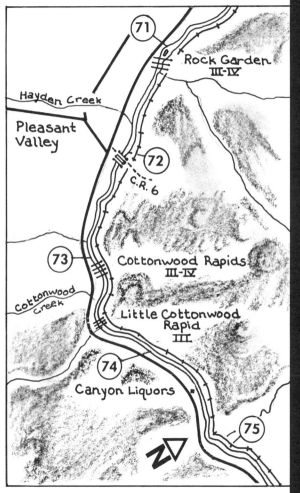

71

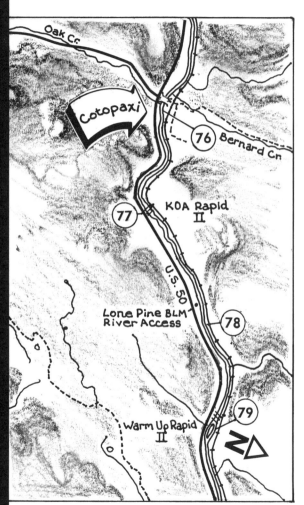

Oak Cr.

Cotopaxi

(76) Bernard Cn

KOA Rapid
II

(77)

U.S. 50

Lone Pine BLM
River Access

(78)

Warm Up Rapid
II

(79)

76

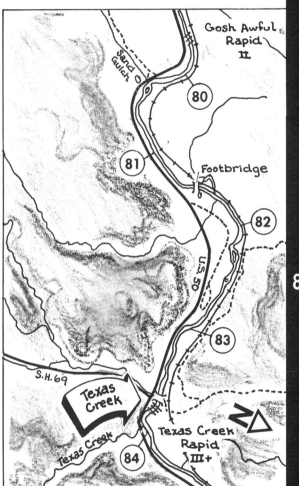

85

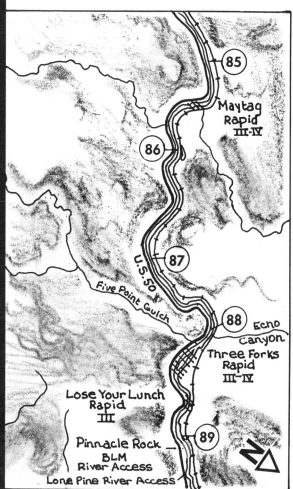

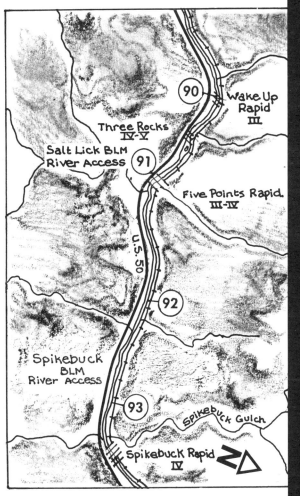

Wake Up
Rapid
III

Three Rocks
IV-V

Salt Lick BLM
River Access

(90)
(91)

Five Points Rapid
III-IV

U.S. 50

(92)

Spikebuck
BLM
River Access

(93)

Spikebuck Gulch

Spikebuck Rapid
IV

90

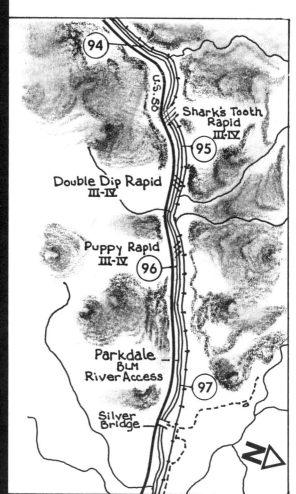

94

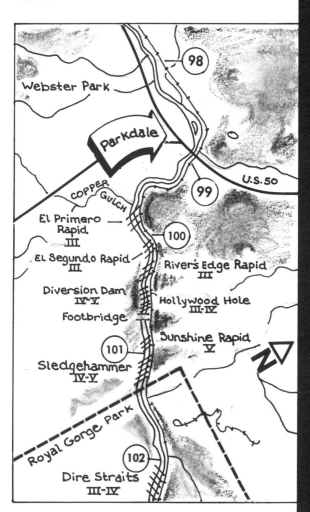

98

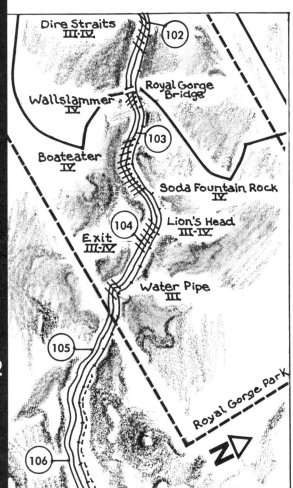

Dire Straits
III·IV

102

Wallslammer
IV

Royal Gorge
Bridge

103

Boateater
IV

Soda Fountain Rock
IV

104

Lion's Head
III·IV

Exit
III·IV

Water Pipe
III

105

Royal Gorge Park

106

102

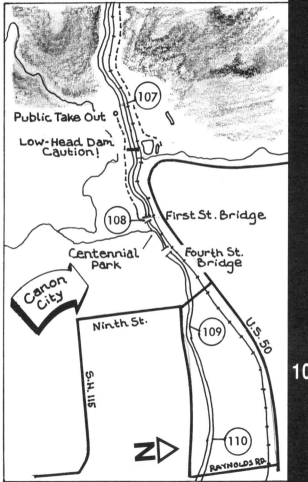

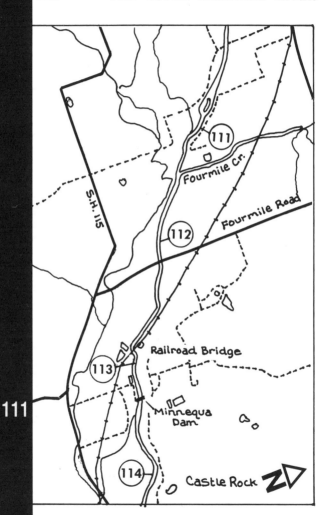

111

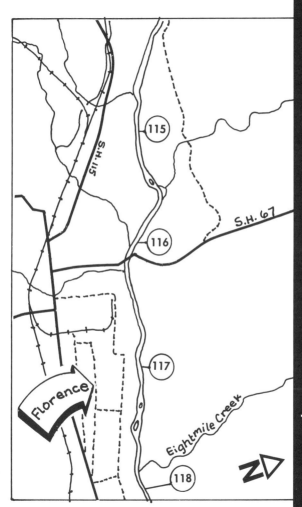

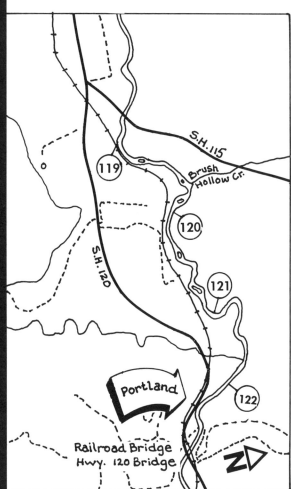

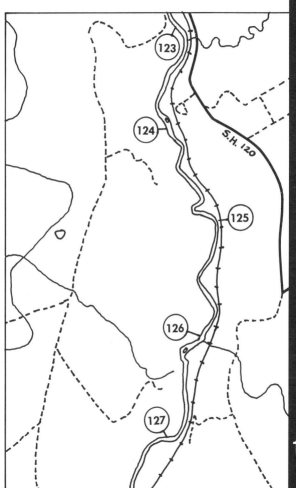

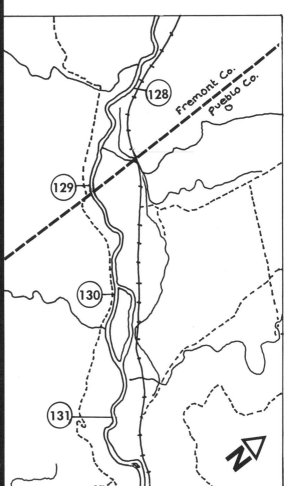

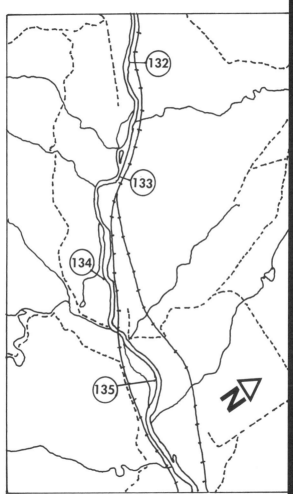

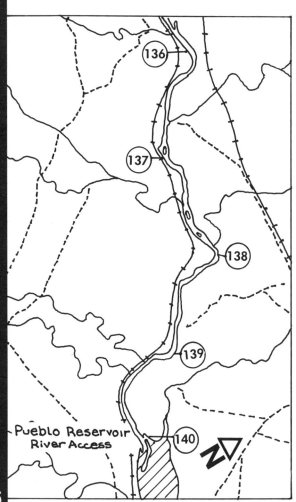

Pueblo Reservoir
River Access

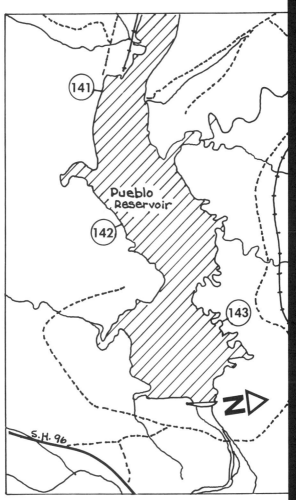

141

Mule deer doe and fawn.

4   POINTS OF INTEREST

The following mile-by-mile descriptions are grouped according to the most commonly run river trips of one-half to one full day as described in chapter 3. The mile numbers appear on the maps. You'll get more out of the following entries by first reading chapter 1 to gain a general understanding of the Arkansas Valley's geology, biology and history. Additional information about a specific subject can be found by referring to the entries indicated by the mile numbers in parentheses. To learn how the various rock formations fit into the geologic time scale refer to table 1, "Geologic History," on page 8 in chapter 1.

Many of the following entries apply to portions of the river which are much larger than that which can be represented by a single mile number. Thus, anyone with a serious interest in learning about the region would do well to read all the entries rather than only those corresponding to the section of river they happen to be traveling.

ABOVE GRANITE: Mile 0 to Mile 6.4

Elevation change: 9180 to 8940 feet above sea level.

Mile 0
Geology

Home of the Fourteeners. Directly west of the Pan-Ark Lodge stands Mount Elbert, which at 14,431 feet is the state's highest peak. Altogether, Colorado has 54 mountains which are at least 14,000 feet high. The exact number changes with each new survey. In the Sawatch Range there are 15 "fourteeners": Massive, Elbert, LaPlata, Huron, Belford, Oxford, Missouri, Harvard, Columbia, Yale, Princeton, Antero, Tabeguache, Shavano and Mount of the Holy Cross. No other mountain range in the country has as many 14,000-foot peaks.

Biology

Destroyed by Fire. From the Pan-Ark Lodge Bridge to Granite, the hills are noticeably devoid of trees, but such was not always the case. During the middle of the last century, the land along this part of the Arkansas did support forests. These were largely destroyed by forest fires, many started by the campfires of careless miners. Many of the trees were also cut for firewood.

Mile 2.4

Biology

Colorado Blue Spruce. This is one of the only places along the river where you can see Colorado's state tree— the blue spruce. Blue spruce are generally found from about 7,000 to 9,500 feet in the moist soil of riparian ecosystems. They are not always blue. Older individuals are often dark green. The most distinguishing field marks are the sharp, stiff needles and the cones which are longer than two and a half inches. Colorado's other spruce, the Engelmann, is usually found at higher altitudes. Its cones are shorter than two and a half inches, and its needles are a bit more flexible.

Mile 4
Geology
Twin Lakes Reservoir. Just north of Highway 82 Lake Creek carries water from Twin Lakes Reservoir into the river. Twin Lakes was originally formed when a glacial moraine dammed Lake Creek.

History
Tragic Train Wreck. On September 6, 1926, a tragic train wreck occurred here. A locomotive, southbound from Leadville, left the tracks on a curve, taking with it several passenger cars. The resulting crash, it was said, could be heard for miles. The engine ended up some 75 feet down-river from the cars, which had formed a bridge across the

This terrible collision occurred near Granite in 1926.
Art Larkin, Buena Vista Heritage Society

river, the coal tender acting as a support.

"When I came on the scene," said one observer, "steam was still issuing from the engine, and continual sizzling caused from the icy water coming in contact with hot steel greeted my ears. Above all this were the screams of mothers, babies, frantic passengers and helpless ones pinned by seats in death chambers formed by coaches that had been smashed like so much tin. It was a ghastly scene—blood covered the wreckage and among the human wreckage were arms, limbs and the flesh of the victims."

Thirty people were killed in the wreck, many of whom were headed home to visit family in Buena Vista for the annual Lettuce Days celebration.

Mile 6.3
Geology
Granite. The town of Granite was named for the principal rock type of the area. Granite is the main component of the continental portions of the earth's crust and is widely used in construction because of its hardness and durability. It forms from quartz-rich molten material deep beneath the earth's surface. The Mosquito Mountains are composed mainly of granite while metamorphic schist and gneiss, in addition to granite, dominate the Sawatches. The boundary between these two major rock types lies along faults beneath the river and the sediments which fill its valley.

History
Granite. A stage stop, as well as several other buildings, was here for nearly a decade before settlers in this area met on July 1, 1868 and unanimously decided to call their

The Town of Granite, as it appeared in the late 1800s.
Buena Vista Heritage Society

town Granite. Granite soon became the county seat in Lake County, and it is said that the county commissioners held their meetings on the top floor of a brewery for many years. At that time, what is now Chaffee County was part of Lake County. Then in February of 1879 the counties divided and Granite was included in Chaffee County.

Granite was a busy mining district in the early days. Some of the more prominent mines on the nearby hillsides were the Yankee Blade, the Belle of Granite and the New Ophir. The name Ophir came from a biblical term meaning a place that contains a lot of gold. More than a few strikes in the area were referred to as the Ophir, prompting one old stage driver to say, "There ain't nothin' out here ceptin' loafer holes, gopher holes, and Ophir holes."

Besides being an outpost for the many prospectors frequenting the hills in the early days, Granite was also an important depot town. Stagecoaches and wagons passing through on their way to Aspen and Leadville frequently stopped in Granite for supplies. Later on, Granite was one of the busiest stations on the Denver–Rio Grande and Colorado Midland railroad lines.

In 1875, Judge E. F. Dyer of Granite issued warrants for the arrest of a number of people who were involved in what has become known as the Lake County War, a dispute surrounding water rights that led to several murders and an attempted lynching. Those summoned to court were heavily armed, and Judge Dyer was assassinated in his own courtroom. The murderer never went to trial.

In the early 1880s, the mining boom in nearby Leadville lured many of the Granite area prospectors away. Nevertheless, a good number of men stayed behind to work on several placer operations in the vicinity of the Arkansas River. Ernest Ingersoll, a traveler and a writer who recorded his impressions of these early days in the Rockies, may well have captured the feel of Granite in the early eighties:

Now we are rapidly approaching Granite, a town twenty-five years old, and presently we catch sight of the great old placers that formerly made the fame of this locality. They are still operated in a quite scientific method and one large flume crosses the track at a height of fully fifty feet. The western bank has been plowed up by water and turned topsy turvy over a long area exposing its innermost pebbles and boulders, all well cleaned up by their second scrubbing.

I reached there too late to attend the proceedings in which it was decided not to hang two Chinamen, whose only crime was that they wanted to come there and work. . . . They left town in a great hurry and that night there was a ball at the Trans-Continental Shades Saloon. . . . The male element predominated in the ball-room. The genial proprietor of the Shades united within himself the duties of both bartender and floor manager.

As for the floor he managed, it was only hard trodden earth, and the decorations of the walls were old coats, old hats, discarded elk antlers, rifles, and some pictures from the Police Gazette in which there was always a sufficient breeze blowing to lift the pretty girl's petty-coats a trifle above her boot tops. . . .

Besides thirty or forty gold washers, rough and big enough to satisfy all conventional requirements for the type, there were present three or four gamblers who set up a faro-table in one corner; the fiddler, a young freightor from Fairplay; and two or three cut-throat Mexicans who had driven up beef cattle from Sa-guache.

By the time the crowd had taken an average of two drinks all around, the bar man ordered the fiddler to "whoop" er up and yelled a general invitation to "clinch". . . . Soon the floor was full of nimble miners, spinning and whirling. The fun continued, tanglefoot whiskey flowing at two bits a drink until everybody was satisfied to go home. I heard the next morning there had been a murder that night; but I do not think that the dance had anything to do with it.

GRANITE CANYON: Mile 6.4 to Mile 8.5
Elevation change: 8940 to 8880 feet above sea level.

Mile 7.1
History

Granite Canyon. Granite Canyon and Pine Creek Canyon offer kayakers some of the most challenging whitewater and dramatic scenery in the state. To traveler Ernest Ingersoll, who wrote several books about the West in the 1880s, the canyon was harsh and desolate:

> Below Granite we pass through a canyon. The inclined and splintered rocks of reddish granite and gneiss rise very high along the eastern bank of the river, and the water itself is in continual ebullition among large boulders, falling meanwhile at such a grade that the train cannot follow it, but must rise away from it.

> The scene here is one of extreme desolation. There is nothing pretty in the whole landscape short of the small snow banks that remind us of scattered sheep browsing on the crest of the range. Almost the only relief to the sterility—sterile not only in respect to pleasing vegetation, but in any comfortable suggestiveness—is when the sun shines suddenly straight down some rift-like gulch in the precipitous walls, transmuting what seemed a crystal clear atmosphere into golden dust finer than any flakes that ever came out of gravels.

Mile 7.9
History

Train Collision. On August 20, 1925 two trains collided at this location. A dispatcher on Tennessee Pass forgot to tell the engineer on the southbound number eight to meet up with the northbound number seven at the depot in Granite.

Earl Roberts, the fireman on number seven's helper engine, was the first to learn of the impending disaster. He looked up from his firebox just in time to see the number eight engine barreling down around a curve not more than 100 yards away. He quickly leapt out of the engine's cab and into the Arkansas River.

His fellow workers weren't quite as lucky. R. T. Willingham, the engineer on the northbound train, rode it out—brakes screaming, wheels grinding on steel rail. The colliding locomotives were totalled, and two of the remaining firemen left on the trains were killed instantly. Willingham managed to emerge from the wreckage, but he was pretty well racked up with 12 broken ribs.

Investigators of the accident gave Willingham and his fellow engineer credit for staying with their trains in an effort to slow them down. The accident, they said, could have been a lot worse. Needless to say, the dispatcher on Tennessee Pass found himself without a job.

PINE CREEK CANYON: Mile 8.5 to Mile 12.4

Mile 8.5
History

Profitable Placers. It was here that A. G. Kelley found gold in the fall of 1859. He pulled out during the winter, returning in the spring of 1860 to set up a mining district surrounding his riverside placer operation. Shortly thereafter, other prospectors reported seeing as many as 25 men working at what came to be known as Kelley's Bar. Kelley's operation and another nearby placer known as Georgia Bar were two of the best producers in the Granite area.

Mile 9
History

Clear Creek. Traveling west on the Clear Creek Reservoir Road, one can see the remains of old mining camps like Vicksburg and Winfield. Both the Clear Creek and Pine Creek mining districts were quite active in 1880, according to the following reports which appeared in the February 8 *Rocky Mountain News:* "On Clear Creek a few miles up from this station, some very rich leads have been struck this winter and the present excitement is high. The report on the train yesterday was that the Roseworth lode near Vicksburg in this district was sold for $70,000 last week."

Former Slalom Course. Ron Maron, a member of the U.S. kayaking team in the early 1970s, once had a slalom course just below Clear Creek where he trained kayakers.

Elevation change: 8880 to 8550 feet above sea level.

Mile 10.4
Geology

Pine Creek Glacial Dam. Thousands of years ago the Pine Creek Glacier and its terminal moraine dammed the river up against the Mosquito Range. On at least two occasions the dam broke, sending floods powerful enough to move great boulders into the valley below. At Pine Creek Rapid, notice the hodgepodge of sand, rocks and boulders in the short cliff face next to the railroad. Unsorted sediments such as these typify glacial deposition.

Mile 10.5
History

Pine Creek. According to a *Rocky Mountain News* article in 1880, "Pine Creek back in the stagecoach days was known as Turkey Creek. . . . The Rio Grande company is now placing an iron bridge across the river at this point. . . [The Pine Creek station] is now the depot for the Pine Creek and Clear Creek Mining districts where some five or six townsites have been surveyed over the past two weeks."

THE NUMBERS: Mile 12.4 to Mile 17.1
Elevation change: 8550 to 8250 feet above sea level.

Mile 12.4
Biology

Sagebrush. Sagebrush dominates the open area adjacent to the OneThrough Six put ins above Scott's Bridge. This species may grow three feet high in some places and is generally found between 7,000 and 10,000 feet above sea level. Sagebrush is a member of the sunflower family (along with asters and daisies), although its flowers certainly don't look like sunflowers to the untrained eye. Sagebrush gets its name from the sage-like odor it emits after a rain. The true sage plant, which is used as a food seasoning, is a member of the mint family. Many animals depend on sagebrush for food and cover. However, cattle prefer the herbaceous plants growing between the bushes. The bare soil caused by heavy cattle grazing is invaded by more sagebrush, resulting in very dense stands. In many parts of the state, big game animals use sagebrush shrublands for their winter range.

Tree Protectors. The glacial boulders lying about the valley floor provide protection for fragile tree seedlings. This is why the ponderosa pine and Douglas firs in the fields near the One Through Six put ins often have rocks at their bases.

Douglas Firs. The dominant trees bordering much of the river above Buena Vista are Douglas firs. The Douglas firs of the Pacific Northwest are enormous, but the colder temperatures, shorter growing season and limited moisture in the Rockies limit Douglas fir growth here to less than 100 feet. Some feel the inland Douglas fir may be a distinct species. Unlike the subalpine fir of higher altitudes, the Douglas fir isn't a true fir and is the only conifer with three-pointed, papery bracts extending from the ends of the cone scales.

Common conifers along the Arkansas.

Mile 13.8
History

Riverside. The settlement of Riverside was located on the west side of the river. Here the Denver and Rio Grande built a depot, section house, bunkhouse and water tank. In 1875, George Leonhardy bought a ranch from Frank Mayol where he ran some cattle, kept hogs, and did a considerable amount of farming, as indicated from this first hand account in the early 1880s:

Mr. Leonhardy has seven miles more or less under cultivation and carries on a highly profitable farm. His extensive hay barns are close to the track and his horse mowers show how scientifically it is cut. All the cereals are grown here or at any rate have been grown; but wheat though it becomes very plump and hard, had so precariously brief a season in which to mature that it is not profitable and hence no great amount is now planted. Of oats, rye and barley, however, hundreds of acres are cut annually, yielding in each case above the average number of bushels to the acre of eastern crops. . . . I have seen some very fine samples of all these grains. Potatoes are particularly successful. . . . Turnips, beets, and onions are doing equally well in their way. . . . Apart from this locality not much farming is visible, except close to Salida.

By 1881, there were several homes in Riverside, and by 1891 there were about 25 active farms and ranches in the vicinity.

FROG ROCK RUN (WILDHORSE CANYON):
Mile 17.1 to Mile 26

Elevation change: 8250 to 7850 feet above sea level.

Mile 21.8
History

Wildhorse and the Midland Tunnels. A small settlement known as Wildhorse (probably because of all the wild horses roaming through the Four Mile Creek area back in the old days) was located near the eastern bank of the river. Originally, Wildhorse was set up as a "helper" station for the Colorado Midland Railroad. Here extra locomotives were kept to help eastbound trains up the steep grade toward Trout Creek Pass. At one time Wildhorse had a frame depot, pump building, wooden water tank, boarding house for railroad crews, cottage for engineers and a railroad repair yard. Nearby, up Four Mile Creek, were the Wildhorse Mines and a mill that processed their ore.

Nothing remains of Wildhorse, but the tunnels just north of the old townsite speak of the Colorado Midland's heyday back in the late 1880s. By the time the Midland crews were bringing track down off of what is now referred to as Midland Hill, the Denver and Rio Grande was already well established. Their right-of-way, squeezing in between the river and the granite outcroppings just north of Wildhorse, forced the Midland engineers to blast out four tunnels in less than four-tenths of a mile.

The Colorado Midland began with the dreams of Homer Fisher, who for years had looked for a better way of transporting lumber from his mill near Woodland Park. With the help of several financial backers, most notably

James Hagerman, a millionaire from Milwaukee, construction began in 1886. By July of 1887, there was passenger service between Colorado Springs and Buena Vista, and by September there was through service to Leadville.

"Two years after construction was begun the high iron was crowded with traffic," wrote Linwood Moody in his story, "The Old Colorado Midland" in the magazine, *Railroad Stories*. "The whole operating force—particularly the engine men and train men—were being taught the true meaning of the word railroading. Never in the history of the country had 2500 tougher miles of standard gauge road been built. Between Buena Vista and Leadville, and Leadville and Basalt, the road went over what was then the highest standard gauge track in America."

Johnny Behind the Rock. There once was a bridge crossing the river in this vicinity. Built for stagecoaches back in 1871, the bridge was destroyed in a fire of unknown origin in 1964. "Another landmark is gone," said a reporter in the *Mountain Mail* (July 9, 1964). "The county maintenance men were called out Sunday to put out a fire on the old stage bridge above Wildhorse. . . . Who was responsible? A careless camper? Vandals perhaps?. . . It was a senseless accident. . . . One person would have been madder than heck about this charred hulk riding at a crazy angle in the river and that was a small bit of a man they used to call 'Johnny Behind the Rock.'"

"Johnny Behind the Rock" was an elderly recluse and prospector who made his home in a rock crevice just north of the old bridge. His shelter consisted of corrugated metal and wood scraps built up against a granite outcropping.

Some said he was a consumptive who had come west to regain his health. Others said he had taken to the hills after being jilted by his bride-to-be. Whatever the case, his life was shrouded in mystery as a result of his reclusive lifestyle. His name apparently came from his habit of hiding behind rocks to avoid contact with strangers. People in the Buena Vista area visited Johnny every now and then, but nobody really knew much about the man and his background.

At times he worked as a section hand for the railroad and held down other temporary jobs in the area, but for the most part he led the life of a pauper. He was often seen wearing gunny sacks for shoes while gathering coal along the railroad tracks, or scavenging for food in town or prospecting along the river.

On a cold December day in 1931, his overalls caught on fire while he was trying to warm himself, and Johnny suffered severe burns. He was taken to the Salida hospital where he died several days later. According to a story in the *Mountain Mail* (December 15, 1931), while at the hospital "He insisted on keeping his overalls under his pillow. In these overalls were found, after his death, bank passbooks showing $1,600 worth of deposits in various bank accounts together with about $25 cash."

Apparently Johnny, whose real name was George Woods, wasn't as destitute as he appeared to be. One of the passbooks showed that he had made deposits under a false name, which led to a great deal of speculation on his personal and financial background. Old-timers in Salida said that a man named George Woods was supposedly killed in a Cripple Creek mining accident in 1903. There were those who believed Johnny was that same man. Others in the Granite area claimed he had sold a sizable amount of gold dust in that town. "There is no telling how much treasure Woods may have accumulated and hidden before his death," said Colorado Attorney General Gail Ireland, who was investigating the matter.

Despite all the theories and speculations, no one ever came up with any hard facts, and "Johnny Behind the Rock" remains a mystery.

Mile 23
Biology

Pinyon Forests. Buena Vista's altitude is almost exactly 8,000 feet, and technically all the land upriver from the town is part of the montane life zone. But as noted in chapter 1, the life zone definition is quite loose, and many of the dry hills along this section of the river are covered with pinyon pine, a tree usually found in the lower foothills. The pinyon forests here are more dense than those in the Arkansas Canyon below 7,000 feet (mile 54.2), probably because of greater soil moisture. As with the ponderosa pine (mile 55.8), pinyon needles occur in bunches of two or three (most true pines have needles in bunches) but pinyon needles are much shorter than those of the ponderosa. Also, ponderosas usually attain greater heights than the short scrubby pinyons.

Mile 23.6
History

Buena Vista. In 1879, David Simonson, a traveling merchant from Canon City, wrote in his journal that Buena Vista had grown into a "town of substantial proportion almost overnight." Shortly after he opened his dry goods store, Simonson said citizens of this fledgling town were circulating a petition for incorporation. With the signatures of 150 inhabitants and 45 qualified voters, and the county judge's seal of approval, Buena Vista found its way onto the map.

By 1880, business was booming, with as many as eight stagecoaches coming through town each day. The coming of the railroads soon gave the town an air of permanence. By February, work crews from the Denver, South Park and Pacific were laying track into town, soon to be followed by the Denver and Rio Grande in June. The Colorado Midland came through later on, in 1887.

Toward the end of 1880, voters in Chaffee County decided to move the county seat from Granite to Buena Vista. The city fathers of Granite, however, were reluctant to give up their town's status, so an enterprising group of some of Buena Vista's more aggressive citizens literally took the matter into their own hands. They borrowed a flat car and an engine, ran up to Granite in the middle of the night, broke into the courthouse and stole all the county records in sight. The next session of county court was held in Buena Vista.

In the mid-1880s, Buena Vista entrepreneurs William Eyre, William Crymble and Walter Telfer initiated the construction of a dam and hydroelectric plant at this location. It was a wood crib dam, and the horizontal water turbine housed in a building on the western bank of the river was generating power as early as 1888. The plant put out enough power for a household to light a 20-watt bulb at each socket, prompting one old-timer to say, "It wasn't bright, but it was light." The Arkansas washed out the original dam in 1910 and the replacement dam in 1952. The power plant put out electricity until 1945.

To the south of the old damsite, near the eastern end of Buena Vista's Main Street, was the old Morley Smelter. Colonel B. F. Morley, who for many years was the superintendent of the famous Mary Murphy Mine up Chalk Creek, fired up his smelter in 1898, much to the delight of those in the mining community. Before this smelter was built, ores were being shipped to Denver and Pueblo for processing. Morley's new operation meant a substantial reduction in shipping costs, and as a result, mining properties that were only marginally profitable in the past now appeared to be better prospects.

Hordes of speculators were soon rushing into the area. "On every train that comes in there are people that have some interest or are looking for a chance to get hold of some property in this part of the state," said a trade journal known as the *Mining Reporter* (October 6, 1898). "It seems as if the old times of the 80s are coming back."

By 1900, however, mining activity was tapering off, and Morley's smelter was working sporadically at best. By 1903, it had shut down. That same year Colonel Morley met an untimely death in the shafts of the Mary Murphy Mine.

According to the *Salida Mail* (September 22, 1903), the colonel "went into the mine to inspect the workings. . . in company with a miner whose name has not been learned. Both men were asphyxiated by gas and died before help could reach them. . . Colonel Morley was one of the best known mining men in Colorado. . . . His death will be a heavy loss to the mining industry and the world at large."

The Lettuce Capital. Water from the upper Arkansas has long been used to moisten the valley's land. But few commercial crops are able to cope with the cool summer nights and short growing season at 8,000 feet above sea level. One of the exceptions is lettuce. Buena Vista once called itself the lettuce capital of the world before California took over the market.

Former Dam Site. Little remains of the Buena Vista Light and Power Company Water Turbine Generating Plant which once stood near the Buena Vista Baseball Field. Between 1888 and 1945 the operation provided enough electricity for a household to burn a 20-watt bulb in each socket. The dam was washed out in 1910, rebuilt and washed out again in 1952.

THE MILKRUN: Mile 26 to Mile 29.6
Elevation change: 7850 to 7720 feet above sea level.

Mile 26
History
Johnson Village. It was here, back in the fall of 1900, that a posse, headed by Sheriff Walker of Buena Vista,

spotted two horse thieves near the banks of the Arkansas. According to the *Denver Republican* (October 7, 1900), Sheriff Walker "as an officer of the law, took part in many of the shooting and lynching affairs that were necessary before the neighborhood of Buena Vista was ridden of its lawless inhabitants. . . . Mr. Walker figured in many exciting hunts after horse thieves, and the cottonwood gulches in the vicinity of Buena Vista furnished the stage settings for the close of more than one earthly drama, in which the main actors were members of Walker's posse and a horse thief, the properties being a sturdy tree and a stout rope."

Walker was rough with all the outlaws in the area, but he was particularly intolerant of horse thieves, the story said. When his posse came onto the thieves, who had apparently been selling stolen horses in Leadville, they gave chase:

The horse thieves were mounted on fine animals, but were finally brought to bay at the head of an impassable draw on the south side of Free Gold Hill [near the present-day KOA campground, approximately at mile 77].

Dismounting, the horse thieves faced their pursuers who were ten in number. There could hardly be but one outcome to such an unequal combat. After a few shots had been exchanged, the taller of the horse thieves fell heavily to the ground. The supposed brother, frenzied at the turn of affairs, fired seemingly without taking aim, until every chamber of the weapon had been emptied. Suddenly, the report of a rifle rang out from an adjacent rock, and the captain of the posse dropped his revolver, a heavy bullet having crashed through his wrist.

As Mr. Walker's revolver dropped to the ground, the young horse thief uttered a scream of agony and fell. The scream startled the assailants and they drew back momentarily and gazed at each other in horror.

"My God boys, we've killed a woman," cried one of the posse, and regardless of the fact that there was an enemy skulking among the rocks, they rushed forward to the prostrate bodies of the horse thieves. . . . They found the body of a woman laying across that of a man. The glossy hair that had been coiled under the cowboy hat of the young horse thief, had tumbled about her head and shoulders in a cloud. Her left hand still clutched her rifle and a dark red stain on the breast of her rough cowboy shirt and knotted handkerchief showed that the bullet had done its work only too well.

It was afterwards ascertained that the couple were man and wife and that the woman had adopted men's dress for the reason that the costume enabled her to better carry on her work of assisting her husband in his dangerous career. The man and woman were buried where they fell, two granite stones marking the place of their death.

Mile 27
Biology
Wild Rose. The Milkrun is a good place to see the pink flowers of the wild rose during the early part of the summer. Ten species of this shrub are found in the Rockies. The fruit

or "rose hip" stays on the plant through the winter and is consumed by animals. Humans eat rose hips also, either raw or in a tea or jelly. Rose hips are an excellent source of vitamin C.

Mile 27.5
Geology
Stream Deposits. A spectacular cross section of sedimentary deposits is exposed where the river bends against a sheer cliff of unconsolidated rocks and dirt. Note the successive patterns of bedding planes laid down by centuries of criss-crossing stream flow, probably from the time of the ice ages.

BROWNS CANYON: Mile 29.6 to Mile 45.6
Elevation change: 7720 to 7200 feet above sea level.

Mile 29.6
Geology
Mounts Yale, Harvard and Columbia. Near Fisherman's Bridge there are good views of the 14,000-foot-high Collegiate Peaks in the Sawatch Range. The symmetrically pointed peak to the south is Mount Yale. The rounded mountain to the north is the Mount Columbia—Mount Harvard Massif. The 1.75-billion-year-old schist and gneiss which forms these summits is approximately the same age and was once at the same level as the Precambrian rock exposed in the Arkansas' many canyons. It now

towers between 6 and 7,000 feet above the valley floor.

Mile 30
Biology
Alders. Dense alder thickets line much of the shoreline on river right, above Browns Canyon and on both sides of the river below the canyon. Their branches frequently overhang the water, providing boaters with a close look at the small, toothed leaves and woody, cone-like reproductive structures.

Mile 31
Geology
Rainbow Rock. The green and yellow on the large, colorfully striped cliff face on river right a quarter mile past the railroad bridge are lichens (see below). The red is iron oxide or rust. Rainbow Rock was probably once part of the northwest flank of Sugarloaf Mountain, an extinct Tertiary volcano bordering the east side of the river, just past the trout farm. Both Sugarloaf Mountain and Rainbow Rock are composed of rhyolite, a solidified lava which in this case flowed between 20 and 30 million years ago. Like granite, rhyolite contains a good deal of quartz (miles 6.3 and 33.5). However, because molten rhyolite cools quickly after being extruded onto the surface, its mineral crystals are small, resulting in a very fine texture. Molten granite, on the other hand, exists deep beneath the earth's surface and cools slowly. Thus, its crystals have enough time to grow large. This makes the texture of granite noticeably

coarser than that of rhyolite.

Biology

Lichens. The green and yellow lichens on Rainbow Rock are often mistaken for moss. Lichens are actually two plants in one—algae and fungi interwoven to give the appearance of a single organism. The fungus provides structural support for the alga which manufactures food for both itself and the fungus. At least 400 species of lichens grow in Colorado. They come in a variety of colors and generally turn black after death. In Browns Canyon some lichens are orange (mile 89).

Mile 31.6

Geology

Ruby Mountain. Those who named Ruby Mountain apparently confused the garnets it contains with rubies. Both are red but rubies are much more valuable. Rockhounds can still collect gem-quality garnets and lesser quality topaz on the sides of this small mountain at the south end of the Ruby Mountain Campground. Like Rainbow Rock and Sugarloaf Mountain, Ruby Mountain is principally composed of rhyolite. Notice the vertical fractures in the cliff above the large talus slope on Ruby Mountain. Vertical jointing such as this is a common characteristic of volcanic rock. It results from shrinkage during cooling.

Mile 32.2

Geology

Chalk Creek. The prominent white cliffs on the southeast side of Mount Princeton are not visible from the river, but they are easily seen from Highway 285. In spite of their name, the chalk cliffs are not chalk but kaolinite. The kaolinite was produced when hot water percolated up through faults and reacted with feldspar, one of the principal minerals in the granite of the Mount Princeton Batholith, a large igneous intrusion (mile 43.5). After a heavy rain on Mount Princeton, suspended kaolinite particles give Chalk Creek the look of watery milk.

Chalk Creek Moraine. Also from Highway 285, look for the long tree-covered hill where Chalk Creek emerges from between Mounts Princeton and Antero. This is a glacial moraine.

History

Chalk Creek. According to a story in the *Mountain Mail* (June 11, 1956), "One Judge Holbrook reported that there was an old Indian fort near Chalk Creek on the Arkansas, but the earliest pioneers do not remember it. They do say, however, that there were high piles of rocks around the place. Every time the Indians passed on their annual trip they moved a rock, some secret signal never discovered by the white man."

When the early Spanish explorers first encountered the Utes, they were based in the San Luis Valley, where buffalo were relatively plentiful at the time. But as the herds thinned out, the Utes went north into the Arkansas Valley and South Park. Both of these areas were considered prime hunting grounds by the Utes and several other tribes, most notably the Comanches and the Apaches, and as a result there were a number of disputes over hunting rights.

By the time the first settlers arrived in the Arkansas

Valley, the Utes were the predominant tribe in the area. Nevertheless, there were still skirmishes with other tribes. Arthur Hutchinson recalled a three-day fight in South Park among the Indians back in 1865. The *Mountain Mail* went on to say, "The victorious Utes celebrated in the Arkansas Valley with much excitement. He says that long after the white people settled in this country, the Utes used signal fires. . . to warn of the approach of the Plains Indians."

There was never any recorded violence between white settlers and the Utes in the Upper Arkansas Valley, although there were a few close calls. Once, for example, a number of Utes stole some army horses from Fort Garland, and the soldiers trailed them into the Upper Arkansas Valley. According to the *Mountain Mail* (June 11, 1956), "Historians believe the place was on the west side of the river below Chalk Creek, where the Indians abandoned the horses when they heard the soldiers coming. They were already back in Fort Garland by the time the soldiers got back with their horses."

Mile 32.5
Biology
Flowers and Birds. One of the finest wildflower areas along the entire Arkansas is on river right, between Chalk Creek and the railroad bridge above Browns Canyon. Monkshood, cow parsnip, mint, daisies and many other species grow here. Flower fields such as this provide good habitat for broad-tailed hummingbirds. Watch for the J-shaped courtship flight of the male. Hummingbirds will sometimes hover around orange life jackets, apparently

mistaking them for the warm-colored flowers from which they draw nectar. Keep an eye out for warblers and gold-finches in this part of the river also.

Mile 33
Biology
Hawks and Muskrats. Red-tailed hawks often ride the thermals just upstream from Browns Canyon. Muskrats have been seen swimming in this area.

Mile 33.5
Geology
Arkansas Hills. Two miles past Ruby Mountain the river takes a sharp bend to the right where it once again contacts the rough country of the southern Mosquito Range, here known as the Arkansas Hills. The hills are a combination of Precambrian granitics and mid-Tertiary volcanics. At this point look back upstream for an inspiring view of Mount Princeton (mile 43.5).

Granitic Gneiss. About 1.75 billion years ago the rock to your left as well as that in most of Browns Canyon existed as hot magma deep beneath the Earth's surface. It cooled very slowly and solidified into granite (an igneous rock). Soon the tremendous pressure from the overlying rock and the intense heat from the Earth's core began to change the granite's crystal structure into that of gneiss (a metamorphic rock). But before the change was complete, the rock was uplifted during the formation of the Rocky Mountains and eventually exposed by erosion. The partially metamorphosed granite you see now is called granitic gneiss.

Black Mica. Rocks are composed of minerals, and granitic rock is typically composed of three minerals: quartz, feldspar and black mica or biotite. In ordinary granite the biotite crystals appear as black specks amid the lighter-colored quartz and feldspar. However, the rock in and around Browns Canyon contains biotite crystals which were made plastic by the intense heat and pressure deep within the Earth. This heat and pressure caused the specks to elongate into streaks (partial metamorphosis). The streakiness identifies the rock as granitic gneiss rather than granite.

Weathering. Like most rocks of igneous origin the granitic gneiss of Browns Canyon (and the Arkansas Canyon downstream) weathers along cracks formed during cooling and by compression when the rock was buried. The edges of the cracks are continually rounded off as weathering by water and frost loosens the mineral crystals. Temperature extremes between day and night and summer and winter also help form the rounded knobs and boulders.

Mile 33.8
Geology

Bumps on the Rock. The granitic gneiss just above and within Browns Canyon is often studded with light-colored bumps. These are especially evident on the boulders approximately one-quarter mile above the railroad bridge. The bumps are feldspar crystals which haven't worn down to the same level as the quartz and mica. Quartz is actually harder and more resistant to erosion than feldspar. But the quartz grains in this formation are generally so small that they break off more quickly than the much larger feldspar crystals.

Mile 34.1
Geology
River Rocks. Note the large piles of river rocks on the left, just upstream from the railroad bridge. Piles such as this suggest the tremendous volumes of water that flowed down the Arkansas when the ice age glaciers melted, some 10,000 years ago. Rocks transported by the river are smooth and rounded from years of wear, while rocks that have recently broken from their bedrock source or were somehow protected from erosion are more angular.

History
Railroad Bridge/Beginning of Browns Canyon. The railroad bridge marks the beginning of Browns Canyon. For the next eight miles or so, the Rio Grande Railroad parallels the river. After two years of battling with the Atchison, Topeka, and Santa Fe Railroad over the right-of-way through the Royal Gorge (mile 99.6), William Jackson Palmer's Rio Grande won a court decision in April of 1880 and began making rapid progress up the Arkansas Valley. By May 14, they had laid track to the Salida area, and by June the line reached to Nathrop.

Old-timers regarded this stretch of rail as one of the most dangerous sections of the Rio Grande line. Train wrecks were not unusual, as indicated in this article from the *Salida Mail* (May 28, 1910): "The 225 went into the river two days ago, within a stone's throw of where Clem and

Hicks had their recent collision, and near the spot where George Jackson scrambled out under the 285, some 18 months previously."

Mile 34.2
Geology

   Browns Canyon. Browns Canyon wouldn't be here if it weren't for the glacial deposits which pushed the river above the Mosquito Range granitics. It may seem odd that the Arkansas didn't bypass this hard rock in favor of the less resistant sediments in the valley floor to the west. But by the time the river cut down to the bedrock, it was probably imprisoned in the channel it had already formed in the softer overlying material and had no other choice. The intense faulting which occurred here no doubt facilitated the cutting of Browns Canyon.

   The Brown Canyon. Browns canyon was originally known as "The Brown Canyon" probably because of the color of the rock. The light brown tone is due to the presence of feldspar which may have changed color due to superheating when it was deep beneath the earth's surface (mile 75.2).

Biology

   Browns Canyon. The foothills are a transition zone between the treeless plains and the high mountain forests. Browns Canyon, which is between 7,000 and 8,000 feet above sea level, is a good example of such a transition because it contains an almost even mix of the dominant plants from the lower montane, foothills and plains environments. Impressive open stands of ponderosa pine occur just above and throughout Browns Canyon. Douglas firs grow in the moister soils while the driest sections support pinyon pine and juniper, or, if conditions are very dry, grasses and shrubs. From a naturalist's standpoint, transition environments such as this are very important places because of their broad diversity of life. Perhaps the government recognized this fact when they decided to protect a one- to two-mile wide swath of the Arkansas Hills from Ruby Mountain through the east side of Browns Canyon and down to the land across from Hecla Junction as a Federal Wilderness Study Area. More likely, the land received this designation because of its limited value for timber and minerals. Browns Canyon and its four-mile approach are good places to see many kinds of wildlife, including the west's most common game species, the mule deer. Dawn is generally the best time to see wildlife.

Mile 35
Biology

Red Flowers. The tubular, red-flowered plants growing on the dry hillsides are one of two possible species: scarlet gilia or firecracker penstemon. From the river it may be difficult to tell them apart. The five petals of the penstemon are fused together and rounded off at their protruding ends with the lower two petal ends forming a kind of tongue. The petals of the scarlet gilia flower are also fused but the ends are pointed and flare out, suggesting a long trumpet.

Mile 35.3
History

Browns Creek and the Lake County War. Browns Creek joins the Arkansas here, flowing in from the west. Back in 1874, two nearby ranchers got into an argument over Browns Creek water rights, which evolved into what has come to be known as the Lake County War. It all started when Elijah Gibbs went to neighbor George Harrington's ranch, hoping to divert more water toward his own property. Harrington allegedly tried to hit Gibbs with a shovel, prompting Gibbs to fire several shots from his pistol. Harrington subsequently had Gibbs arrested.

Gibbs claimed that his gun had gone off by accident, and his explanation fell on sympathetic ears, as Judge Cowen was his brother-in-law. He then told the judge that his wife was sick at home, and needed tending to. Cowen let him go.

That same night George Harrington's store was set on fire. While he was trying to douse the flames, someone shot him in the back. Because of their earlier disagreement, Elijah Gibbs was a prime suspect. Several days later, he was arrested and hauled off to Denver to stand trial. Having been acquitted by the jury, he returned to the valley, where a number of Harrington's friends, planning to take the law into their own hands, had formed a vigilance committee.

This committee, which at one time numbered as many as 70 men, terrorized a number of Gibbs' sympathizers into leaving the valley. Gibbs himself was preparing to move on when the committee came to his house late one night, apparently with the idea of taking him into custody and hanging him from the nearest tree. Several of the vigilantes tried to smoke him out of his ranch house, whereupon Gibbs opened fire, seriously wounding Sam Boon, Boon's brother David, and their uncle Finly Kane. These men were taken to a log house on the west side of the Arkansas near Browns Creek, where they finally died. In the meantime, Gibbs managed to escape to Colorado Springs.

When Sheriff Weldon finally caught up with him in Denver, Gibbs was in the protective custody of several Denver law officers. They refused to surrender Gibbs and he was never seen in the valley again. Despite his disappearance, violence stemming from the vigilante committee continued well into 1875. In February of that year, Colorado governor John Jenkins issued a proclamation calling for "the lawless people of Lake County to disperse." Later on that spring, County Judge E. F. Dyer of Granite tried to take action through the courts, issuing warrants for several committee members. They arrived in court heavily armed and were apparently dismissed based on a lack of evidence.

Following the trial, the Lake County War culminated with the murder of Judge Dyer. "The judge was sitting in an office chair, and three or four shots were fired," wrote his father, Reverend John Dyer, in *The Snowshoe Itinerant*. "One man on the outside heard him cry, 'Spare my life,' but he must have made toward them and been caught by some of them near the door, as the pistol was evidently put close to his head."

No one ever went to trial.

Mile 37
Biology

Contrasting Environments. The north-facing cliff on river left at the top of Staircase Rapid is shaded during the morning. This keeps evaporation to a minimum so the soil there remains relatively moist, favoring the growth of tall Douglas firs. In contrast, the sunny south-facing slope directly across the river loses so much water through evaporation that only drought-resistant species such as pinyon pines, junipers and ponderosa pines can survive.

Mile 37.8
Geology

Evidence of a Fault. Immediately after the Toilet Bowl note the flat-sloping rock surface on river right. It was scraped smooth by movement along a fault above which the river now flows for a short distance. Geologists call these kinds of structures slickensides.

Mile 37.9
Geology

Gneiss. After House Rock in Widowmaker look quickly to the left just above the water level for a wall of heavily banded or foliated metamorphic rock polished to a shine by the river. Millions of years ago this rock existed deep beneath the Earth's surface where intense heat and pressure caused the minerals to sort themselves into bands. Rock which has been metamorphosed to this extent is true gneiss as opposed to granitic gneiss in the rest of Browns

Canyon (mile 33.5). Most of the rock on river left from Widowmaker Rapid to Hecla Junction is gneiss as evidenced by its banding. NOTE: The pink boulders on river left a short distance downstream were hauled in by the railroad from somewhere else in order to shore up the bank. Some of these boulders are sandstone and and some are pegmatite (mile 74.5).

Mile 38
Geology
Jigsaw Rock. Approximately a quarter mile past Widowmaker and just upriver from "Jump Rock," a Volkswagen-sized piece of granitic gneiss lies on its side five feet above the water on river right. As you pass this bullet-shaped boulder notice that its left-hand end is the perfect jigsaw puzzle match to the top of an equally large rock immediately downstream. Judging from the eroded contours on the top of the downstream rock the two must have split from each other many thousands of years before. Somehow their positions shifted after the parting.

Napkin Ring Rock. Immediately after Jigsaw Rock look quickly to the left for a boulder with a hole through its middle (covered during very high water). Most of the erosive work the river does on hard rock such as this occurs only during periods of heavy runoff when great quantities of suspended sand and gravel rasp at the canyon floor. At the end of the last ice age the erosive power of the river must have been tremendous as floods of glacial melt water passed through the canyon with their loads of abrasive sediment.

Biology

Self-Planting Plants. In late summer, feathery tails on
the seeds of a large shrub called mountain mahogany cause
a white glow to appear around its branches. When a seed
falls, the tail acts like a parachute, keeping the seed head
facing down so that it strikes the dirt first. Changes in
humidity then cause the tail to alternately bend and
straighten out. In this way, the tail acts like an auger, drilling
the seed into the soil. A long filament extending from the
seed of needle and thread grass has the same function. The
sharply-pointed needle and thread grass seeds frequently
become lodged in the socks of hikers and river travelers.
You may see these plants close up if you stop for lunch in
the area around Jump Rock.

Possible Porcupine Sign. Just past Jigsaw, Napkin
Ring and Jump Rock on river right, notice the bare spots at
the base of the ponderosa pines next to the river. These may
be scars from rocks tumbling along the shore during high
water, but they bear a strong resemblance to the sign left by
porcupine feeding on the trees' soft inner bark.

Mile 38.3
Biology

Mullein. The stalked plants along the railroad in the
long calm stretch above Raft Ripper Rapid are mullein, also
known as Indian Toilet Paper because of the usefulness of
their large, soft leaves. Being an exotic, mullein grows best
in disturbed soil where the native vegetation has been
destroyed.

Mile 38.7
Biology

Growing Out of the Rock. The small tree growing out of a crack in the large boulder on river right midway between Raft Ripper Rapid and Hecla Junction is a ponderosa pine. In a semiarid environment such as this, trees and other plants actually gain an advantage by growing in rock cracks as well as next to cliffs and large boulders. When rain comes, it runs off the rock and collects in the thin strip of soil supporting the plants. In this way, the roots receive an extra measure of water.

Mile 39
History

Why All The Wires? Boulders tumbling down off the canyon walls and onto the railroad tracks were the cause of several train wrecks in this vicinity, one of which was described in the *Salida Mail*, in December of 1939:

> The boulder . . . estimated to weigh between thirty and forty tons . . . blocked the track only a few minutes before the train came to a curve near Hecla Junction. The engineer was unable to see the slide until they were right on it. The rock, which broke loose from a ledge 250 feet above the tracks, took out a twelve foot section of rail.
>
> After the engine struck the rock and derailed, it turned over on its side. Two baggage cars and the mail car were derailed but did not overturn. . . Engineer William Reardon suffered from severe scalds and burns from inhaling super heated steam . . . Fireman Nemier

received painful bruises on the head, a broken nose, and a large cut on his forehead.

The injured men were assisted to a Pullman car. They were in a dazed condition and were given first aid immediately by Miss Ferrel Mitchell, who at this time was returning to Salida from Leadville. The injured men were moved to Browns Canyon Depot, where Costello's ambulance was waiting to take them to the Denver and Rio Grande Hospital in Salida.

Mr. Nemier survived. Reardon, the *Mail* said, "had been in various railroad accidents of almost every conceivable kind, always managing to escape with minor injuries. He is the oldest engineer in point of service on the road." This time Reardon's luck ran out. He died several days after the accident.

Today, such mishaps are guarded against by a system of wires strung across the cliff face next to the track. If a rock breaks through a wire and falls onto the track, a signal is transmitted to warn approaching trains.

Mile 39.1
Geology
The Black Sand Has the Gold. Hecla Junction is a popular gold-panning spot. While few ever strike it rich, some modern-day prospectors are able to pay for their vacations with their hobby. The gold is found in the black sand which forms a band at the water's edge atop the pale, light-weight quartz sand. The black sand contains heavy minerals (mostly magnetite), allowing it to be isolated in a pan. The few tiny flecks of gold can be separated from the

black sand later, either chemically or with a tweezers. Don't confuse the many shiny specks on the sand and in the water with gold. They're usually just tiny flakes of mica and perhaps a bit of fool's gold (iron pyrite).

Mile 40
History

Railroad Gulch. Railroad Gulch, just to the east of the river, was a busy place back in June of 1880. About 50 men were at work, grading out what was to become the Calumet Branch of the Denver and Rio Grande Railroad. Tracks were to be laid up the gulch to mining properties owned by the Colorado Coal and Iron Company (which later became the CF&I Steel Corporation of Pueblo).

This company owned 62 acres of claims including the Calumet, the Hecla and the Smithville—which made up what was known as the Calumet Iron Mine—the only iron mine in the state at the time.

By November of 1880, the spur line up to Calumet was complete. On November 20, the first train made the trip up to the mine—a distance of seven miles, with an elevation gain of about 1,500 feet.

Conquering what on the average was a 7 percent grade was truly a great achievement, prompting one writer to describe the Calumet Branch as "the perpendicular railroad." One of the workers on the line said that hiring out to run the Calumet was called 'carrying the hod'. . . for it's about as near a ladder as anything you ever saw. . . . This branch is so popular with officers of the Rio Grande that only two of them ever made the ride from the clouds to the earth." The same railroader said that the trip up to the mines took an hour and a half, while the trip down was made in 15 minutes.

One story (perhaps more folklore than it is fact) that has come down through the years concerns an engineer by the name of Abe "Hardluck" Leonard. Cy Warman, in his story "Abe Leonard's Wild Ride," said that Leonard was on his way down the Calumet on a snowy September day, when he ran into problems:

> The rail was wet and slippery for the snow was melting as it fell. Leonard knew the danger of a greasy rail and was proceeding very cautiously. The locomotive at times would hold the train with what is known as the water brake but presently the sand gave out, or the pipes got stopped up at the bottom with wet snow, and the engine slipped and lurched and broke away from the train. . . .

> The conductor and the three brakemen were on top of the train (a man to each car and brake set on the caboose), but before they could tighten up the hand brakes, the heavy ore cars hit the floundering locomotive and sent her down the track, like a sled on a slide. . . . The firemen who had been standing on the gangway were thrown off by the force of the collision and Leonard was left alone with the helpless locomotive. . . .

> The runaway engine was nearing the junction of the main line which ran at right angles with the branch line along the Arkansas. (By this time Leonard was saying his prayers.) As the engine neared the river, he stood in the gangway and the moment she left the bank

he leaped, or threw himself clear, and lit in the middle of the stream. Dazed momentarily by cold water, within minutes he made it to shore.

Whether Leonard's story is true is open to speculation, but the fact remains that the Calumet Branch of the Rio Grande was one of a kind. "That little branch," said the *New York Times* (November 2, 1884), "has the heaviest curves (22 percent) and the steepest grades (406 feet or 7 percent per mile) of any railroad in the world that used the ordinary drivewheel locomotives to run its cars."

Over the years, the Calumet Branch, like the mines it was serving, ran sporadically. Then in August of 1901 a serious flood tore up the tracks and bridges, putting the Calumet out of commission once and for all. All that remains are a few steel rail scraps hidden away, up the gulch.

Mile 40.5
History

Seidel's Suckhole. Seidel's was named for German kayaker Erich Seidel. A member of the Munich Kayaking Club, he was one of many Europeans who came to participate in Salida's FIBArk boat race in the early days of the race (mile 51). In 1953, along with Theo Bock (also from Munich), Seidel set up the first slalom course included in the FIBArk festivities. That same year he won the down-river race, but declined the $1,000 cash prize in order to retain his amateur status.

Mile 40.6
Biology

Bighorn Sheep and Mountain Goats. Bighorn sheep may be spotted among the cliffs and talus slopes on river left from Seidel's Suckhole, past Twin Falls, to an area across from the old Fluorite Mill. Bighorn once ranged all the way down to the edge of the plains but their sensitivity to human intrusion has now limited them largely to the wilderness. Mountain goats, on the other hand, have never lived anywhere but in the alpine and subalpine life zones and are thus never seen along the river. In Colorado, mountain goats were imported as an additional game animal. They were first introduced on Mount Shavano in the Sawatch Mountains directly to the west. Today, the Sawatch Range contains the state's largest mountain-goat herd (miles 55.8 and 89.4).

Mile 41
Geology

Fluorite. Behind the cottonwood trees on river right, a half mile past Twin Falls, are the buildings of a fluorite processing mill which operated at the beginning of this century. For a good view of the mill (which stands on private property) look back upstream while passing through the riffles next to the reddish volcanic rock at mile 41.2. The mill was supplied by mines along the road to Hecla Junction and at other locations in Browns Canyon. Fluorite is used as a flux in steel making and as an ingredient in hydrofluoric acid.

Bighorn sheep ram.

Mile 41.2
Geology

   Wall Mountain Volcanics. Near the end of Browns Canyon the river leaves behind the gneiss and granitic gneiss and passes through more rhyolite from the Tertiary volcanic episodes. The rhyolite's best exposure is on river right, a short distance past the fluorite mine. Note its rougher, redder and vertically jointed appearance. In this case the rhyolite originated as part of the Wall Mountain ash flows which exploded from a source near Mount Aetna to the west some time between 28 and 35 million years ago. Ash flows are suspended particles of frothy magma spewed from a volcano in a stream of hot gases. The Wall Mountain volcanics covered an extensive area from South Park to the Wet Mountain Valley and eastward across the present Rampart Range and out onto the plains at least as far as Castle Rock. The thickness of the formation ranges from about 100 to 500 feet (mile 65.9).

Mile 42.5
Biology

   Swallow Nests. After leaving Browns Canyon you'll probably have to duck to get under Stone Bridge, but don't forget to look up. The bridge's underside supports a colony of cliff swallows which may shoot out from their globular mud nests within inches of passing boats. Swallows fly like stunt planes enabling them to catch insects on the wing (mile 123).

Mile 42.5
Geology
More Valley Fill and More Volcanics. After leaving Browns Canyon the river once again winds through soft material eroded from the mountains. These sediments are part of either the Dry Union Formation (mile 45.6) or younger glacial outwash. If you climb to the top of the river's east bank you'll be able to see red-colored deposits from the Wall Mountain volcanic episode bordering the Arkansas Hills (miles 33.5 and 41.2).

Biology
Owls, Kingfishers, Mergansers and Kestrels. Below Stone Bridge more examples of fine riparian habitat line much of the river. Keep an eye out for great horned owls sitting in the cottonwoods and alders. Kingfishers are especially common in this part of the river (mile 58.9). Boaters sometimes come upon a merganser or two here as well as in the lower part of Browns Canyon. Kestrels or sparrow hawks often hover over the nearby flatlands in search of small prey.

Mile 43.5
Geology
Mounts Shavano, Antero and Princeton. After the Highway 291 Bridge some excellent views of the southern Sawatches open up. Mounts Shavano, Antero and Princeton, all over 14,000 feet, can be seen. These peaks were formed mainly from a circular intrusion of hot molten granite which solidified during the Tertiary Period (mile

32.2). This rock is thus much younger than the Precambrian schist and gneiss of Mounts Yale, Harvard and Columbia and the rest of the Sawatches to the north (mile 29.6).

Glaciers and Snowfields. Glaciers still exist in Colorado but not in the Sawatch or Sangre de Cristo Ranges. However, the peaks visible from the river are spotted with snowfields, some of which may last the summer. Snowfields are mostly snow while glaciers have been compacted into ice. Also, a glacier's slow movement downhill may cause its surface to split into dangerous crevasses. Snowfields do not move and their surface is unbroken. They form in shaded areas or in gullies and depressions where the snow accumulates, as with the Angel of Shavano.

History

The Angel of Shavano. The snowfields in the cirque of Mount Shavano, visible off to the west during most of the year, have long been referred to as the Angel of Shavano. The Angel is in her best form during the early part of the river season. By mid-July her head and right arm have usually melted away.

In Tabeguache Ute legend, the angel was known as the snow spirit. According to the legend, two Ute chiefs, Stone Face and Little Drum, were to have a duel in order to win the love of an Indian princess known as Corn Tassel. Before the showdown, Corn Tassel told Little Drum, the man she truly loved, to take her life if he found himself losing the fight. Holding to that agreement, he shot an arrow through her heart, as he fell to his knees with an arrow through his own breast.

With the princess's death, hard times fell upon the tribe. Crops withered in drought. People were starving. The tribal leaders decided that it was time to seek out a new home. One morning, as they made their way through the Arkansas Valley, they looked up toward the west and saw the image of the princess on the side of a mountain.

They interpreted this to be a good sign. Her spirit, they felt, would watch over them, and the valley would be fertile. As time passed they found themselves enjoying a bountiful harvest, and the Arkansas Valley became their new home.

The Arkansas Valley was indeed home to the Utes for many years, and a number of peaks in the Sawatch Range have been named in their honor. Shavano was named for a well-known Ute leader, as was Mount Ouray, one of the more prominent peaks to the south. To the north and west of Ouray are Chipeta and Pahlone, which were named for Ouray's wife and son, respectively.

A very different legend about the Angel of Shavano has its basis in classical mythology and was reported in a 1984 summer publication of the Salida *Mountain Mail*. According to the late Corrinne Harpending, Jupiter was angered by the pranks of a young goddess and changed her into an angel of white ice, saying: "Until some mishap or tragedy of other people moves you to tears, you will remain on Mount Shavano." For many years the people in the valley below the angel prospered and she was content. Then a drought dried up the river and caused much hardship. This made the angel cry. As her tears fell on her body, the snow and ice melted. The melt water flowed down into the valley, filling the river and restoring the health of the people. Just before she melted away completely she heard a voice say: "Angel of Shavano, you have served your people well. In cold months of the year you will stand there as before, but when the warm winds come you will send your icy body down to aid your people."

Mile 44
Biology
Cottonwoods. Cottonwoods are relatively abundant along the river between Browns Canyon and the Arkansas Canyon because of the broader floodplains. The narrowleaf cottonwood is the common cottonwood in the upper foothills, as well as in higher life zones. In the lower foothills and plains it is replaced by the plains cottonwood which has broad triangular leaves like those of an aspen. (Cottonwoods and aspens are both in the poplar family.) Where the ranges of the narrowleaf and plains species overlap they may interbreed to produce the lanceleaf cottonwood which has a leaf intermediate in shape between that of its parents. Cottonwoods get their name from the white cotton-like fluff that allows the seeds to be carried by the wind (mile 65.3).

Mile 45
History
Zebulon Pike Camps Near Squaw Creek. Squaw Creek joins the river here, flowing in from the west. In 1806, Lieutenant Zebulon Pike and his exploration party spent Christmas in this vicinity. Pike and his men came into

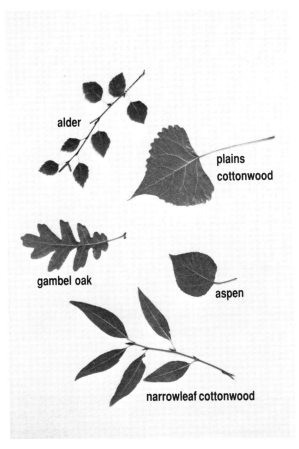

Common deciduous trees along the Arkansas.

South Park from what is now the Pueblo area, eventually crossing Trout Creek Pass and dropping down into the Arkansas Valley. At this point, Pike divided his party into two groups, one which would travel toward the headwaters of the river (which he mistook for the Red River), leaving the other group to explore downstream.

Heading upstream from Trout Creek, Pike and his half of the party probably camped somewhere between the old townsite of Riverside and Granite. At one point, they may have gotten as far north as the Twin Lakes area. "Marched up 13 miles to a large point of mountain from whence we had a view of at least 35 miles to where the river entered the mountains," he wrote, "it being at that place not more than 10 or 15 feet wide, and properly speaking only a brook."

Heading south, Pike found signs of the other party somewhere in the vicinity of Chalk Creek. "Discovered the trace of the party on the opposite side of the river," he wrote. "We forded it, although extremely cold and marched some time into the night. When we arrived at the second night's encampment of the party, our clothing was frozen stiff and we ourselves were considerably benumbed."

On the following day, December 24, 1806, Pike and his men were reunited with the rest of the expedition near Squaw Creek. "Sent out horses for the meat, shortly after Sparks arrived and informed us that he had killed four buffalo. Thus from being in a starving condition, we had eight beeves in camp. We now again found ourselves together on Christmas eve and appeared generally to be content, although all the refreshment we had to celebrate that day with was buffalo meat without salt or any other thing whatever."

Feasting on buffalo must have bolstered the spirits of Pike's party, since they hadn't eaten for several days. Historians believe that the buffalo disappeared from the Arkansas Valley sometime between Pike's Christmas here in 1806 and the coming of the prospectors in 1860. According to the reminiscences of several early settlers, the winter storms of 1840 killed off most of the herd.

Geology

What Causes Whitewater? (Squaw Creek Rapid). Rapids result from a variety of factors. Steep gradients, abundant rocks, sudden drop-offs, and narrow channels may work separately or in combination to create exciting whitewater. The waves in Squaw Creek Rapid are partly the result of rocky debris washed into the river by flash floods coming out of Squaw Creek. The steep gradient and sharp bend at this point in the river are also responsible for the rapids' formation.

Mile 45.6

Geology

Dry Union Formation. As the second major uplifting of the Rockies subsided in the latter part of the Tertiary Period about 12 million years ago, erosion products from the mountains accumulated atop the Precambrian basement rock of the Rio Grande Rift to form the Dry Union Formation. This layer of sandstone, claystone and unconsolidated material underlies much of the Arkansas Valley and may be over 15,000 feet thick in some places. Many of the sparsely vegetated hills between the river and the Sawatch Mountains were cut from the Dry Union. But its most impressive exposure is in the cliffs above Adobe Park near the section of river known as Big Bend. These sediments are much older than those washed down from the valley glaciers of the Quaternary Period.

THE SALIDA RUN:
Mile 45.6 to Mile 54.3

Elevation change: 7200 to 6950 feet above sea level.

Mile 46.8
History

Gypsy Divers. Near this spot in 1985 William Taylor died while participating in the Larry Hill Memorial Race. The eight-mile race is held each June during FIBArk (mile 51) by the Colorado Gypsy Divers and is open to experienced river swimmers equipped with masks, snorkels and wetsuits. Taylor was knocked unconscious when he struck his head on a rock or log and drowned. At one time the race began at Squaw Creek but the starting line was later moved downriver to Adobe Park in order to avoid Squaw Creek Rapid (mile 45). The F Street Bridge in Salida is still the finish line. Larry Hill, a Salida diver for whom the race was named, was the race's first organizer. He also died tragically in an auto accident. Since 1965 the Gypsy Divers have positioned themselves along the river bank during the various FIBArk races in order to make rescues.

Gypsy divers.
Photo by David Lichtenstein

Mile 49.3
History

Smeltertown Dam. The dam was built to insure an ample water supply for the fish hatchery at mile 49.8. Water pouring over the dam creates an extremely dangerous keeper-type suckhole at its bottom. In 1987, a canoeist drowned while trying to navigate the dam. At the time of this writing, the construction of a chute is being discussed to allow for the safe passage of boats through this most treacherous spot on the Arkansas.

Mile 49.5
History

Smeltertown. The brick smokestack, visible off to the east of the river, looms over what at one time was the community of Kortz, later called Smeltertown. In the early 1900s, the Ohio Colorado Smelting Company was busy processing ores from mines in the area. In 1916, local residents complaining about the smoke from the company's stacks claimed that their farmland and livestock were being contaminated.

They filed suit against the company and won. Forced to pay damages, the company decided to solve the pollution problem by building a taller smokestack. This 364-foot stack, which required 262 rail-car loads of bricks, was finished in 1917.

It was built on a 40-foot-wide cement foundation that went 30 feet underground, down to the granite bedrock. Standard gauge railroad tracks were encased in the concrete base to lend vertical support to the structure. Construction costs amounted to $43,000 back then. Today, it is estimated, a similar project would cost two million dollars.

In 1973, the old smokestack was the center of a heated controversy. The Chaffee County Commissioners announced their plans to sell the smokestack (the smelter property had fallen into county hands after the operation shut down in 1919) to Columbine Minerals Company. After hearing that the company would demolish the stack, historically minded locals, refusing to stand by and watch an old landmark disappear, formed a committee known as S.O.S. (Save Our Stack).

They filed suit against the county commissioners, claiming that the commissioner had sold the property without regard for its historical significance. Because Columbine was the only bidder, they said, it was not in the county's best interest to sell the property. The court date was set for August 29.

"The fate of the historic Smeltertown Smokestack on the outskirts of Salida remains in doubt today," said the *Mountain Mail* (August 25, 1973), "with a court hearing into the lawsuit aimed at preventing its scheduled demolition August 29, and with reports rife in the community that the firm which holds title to the ground on which the stack stands has plans to tear it down on the 28th — one day short of the scheduled court date with District Judge Howard Purdy."

During this time, S.O.S. members took turns "standing guard" out at the stack. Finally, the trial was held, but after Judge Purdy's ruling in favor of the commissioners, it appeared that the old stack was doomed. Then came a surprising turnaround on the part of the Columbine management. Company president Jack Lafollette called S.O.S. chairman Wendall Hutchinson, telling him that his company would donate the stack to a responsible organization, if they could be assured of getting a tax write-off.

With the help of the Salida city council, S.O.S. members worked out the details and the deal was finalized. Ownership of the smokestack was subsequently transferred to the Salida Museum Association. It is now on the National Register of Historic Places.

Mile 49.8
History

Fish Hatchery. Between 1925 and 1953, Horace Frantzhurst owned the fish hatchery on the right side of the river. At one time it was the largest privately owned trout farm in the world, and Frantzhurst was selling thousands of trout to railroad dining cars, restaurants and cafes in this part of Colorado.

In 1956, the state purchased the hatchery from the Small Business Administration for $135,000. According to a Division of Wildlife brochure, "It produces 284,000 pounds of nine-inch fish with a total production of 345,000 pounds per year at a cost of 68 cents a pound. The unit annually hatches six million eggs of species such as rainbow, cutthroat, and brown trout."

Mile 51
History

Salida. While the Atchison, Topeka and Santa Fe and William Palmer's Denver and Rio Grande Railroads were embroiled in a controversy over right-of-way through the Royal Gorge (mile 97.5), a small settlement known as Cleora (mile 54.2), several miles downstream from present-day Salida, was taking shape. Officials of the Atchison, Topeka and Santa Fe had surveyed the area for a future townsite, and speculative entrepreneurs were setting up businesses in anticipation of the coming railroad.

Then, on April 4, 1880, a court decision returning the Royal Gorge right-of-way to the Denver and Rio Grande in effect determined Cleora's fate. The Denver and Rio Grande officials had no intention of developing their rival's townsite. They purchased ranch land farther upstream, founding the townsite of South Arkansas (later to become Salida).

By May 1, 1880, Rio Grande crews were laying track into town. By May 20, South Arkansas had its own railroad station. The first bank opened its doors on June l, and the first newspaper hit the streets on June 5. Joe King was building a saloon, scrounging building materials from the railroad yard. Those who had originally settled in Cleora were taking their businesses and moving upstream. Within several months, South Arkansas had two furniture stores, two barber shops, a drug store, a hardware store and a clothing and dry goods business.

By October 4, the town was incorporated. Governor Hunt and his wife, having recently returned from a trip to Mexico, were riding a passenger train up the Arkansas River when they came up with the name Salida—a Spanish word meaning exit or gateway. Salida was first and foremost a railroad town. Over the years the Rio Grande developed Salida into a major division point on their line, complete with a sizable roundhouse and repair yard. In addition to employing many of Salida's early residents, the Rio Grande contributed to the town's development when they built a hospital and a well-known hotel known as the Monte Cristo.

Today, the Denver and Rio Grande's presence in Salida is a mere vestige of what it once was, and many of the classic railroad structures which the Salidans had come to cherish as civic landmarks have gone under the bulldozer. But according to the National Historic Register, Salida still has some of the best turn-of-the-century architecture in Colorado. Also, Salida is the state's largest National Historic District.

The First FIBArk. Salida's annual FIBArk downriver kayak race starts near here. Two Salida businessmen, who also happened to be boating enthusiasts, were responsible for FIBArk's creation in 1949. What started off as a story-telling session centering around various river-running achievements evolved into a challenge to race from Salida to Canon City.

Before long, Chamber of Commerce members from each of the towns were pitching in to organize the event. "Members of the Salida branch of Colorado's fastest-grow-

The start of the 1987 FIBArk downriver kayak race.

ing navy will meet with Chamber of Commerce members in Canon City," said the *Mountain Mail* (May 3, 1949) "to draw up rules and regulations for the fleet's big event." They decided that racers could run the boat of their choice as long as they didn't use sails or motors. They also agreed that racers could portage when necessary.

A fleet of 23 boats took off down river on race day in 1949. Two Salida amateurs, Bill Anderson and Paul Pasquale, racing in a boat they had fashioned from an airplane belly gas tank, had to jump ship when they couldn't get their boat to shore for the first portage. J. Kessner, national amateur whitewater champ from Long Island, hit a rock in his fold boat and capsized. Box Wigden and Jim Pickerell of Canon City sank their boat in the Royal Gorge after taking on too much water. John Wells of Thermopolis, Wyoming, made it 21 miles before his metal canoe got so beat up he had to pull out.

The only team to cross the finish line that year was Robert Ris and Max Romer, two young Swiss racers, who came into Canon City with a time of seven hours and eighteen minutes. The race, they said, had been more of an endurance course than a test of boating skills. With that in mind, the FIBArk committee decided to shorten the race the following year, excluding the Royal Gorge.

Nowadays, FIBArk, which stands for First in Boating on the Arkansas, consists of a slalom race, held in the vicinity of the F Street Bridge, and a downriver race which runs from Salida to the Cotopaxi bridge, a distance of about 26 miles. There are separate divisions for kayaks and rafts. A short Hooligan Race is also held. Anything that floats may be entered in the Hooligan Race as long as it isn't a boat. Foot races, bicycle races and a variety of other events are also held during the four-day FIBArk celebration. FIBArk is usually held the third weekend in June to coincide with high water.

TABLE 4—PAST WINNERS OF THE FIBARK 26-MILE DOWNRIVER RACE

Year	Name	Home	Time
1949	Robert Ris, Max Romer	Basel, Switzerland	7:18:13
1950	Clyde Jones	Denver, CO	10:50:40

1951	Bob Ehrman	Cloverdale, CA	2:56:22
1952	Bob Ehrman	Cloverdale, CA	3:10:52
l953	Erich Seidel	Munich, W. Germany	3:04:02

note: before 1954 the course varied in distance

1954	Roger Paris	Orleans, France	2:54:41
1955	Rudy Pillwein	Austria	2:05:20
l956	Roger Paris	Orleans, France	2:24:01
1957	Rudolph Klepp	Vienna, Austria	2:05:20
1958	Roger Paris	Orleans, France	2:26:35
1959	Laurence Campton	Salida, CO	2:23:59
1960	Eduard Kahl	Vienna, Austria	2:19:33
1961	Dan Makris	Salida, CO	2:42:14
1962	Rudi Gruenburg	Munich, W. Germany	2:12:33
1963	Dan Makris	Salida, CO	2:42:14
1964	Siegi Gunzenberger	Rosenheim, W. Ger.	2:20:35
1965	Franz Heiber	Leoben, W. Germany	2:03:08
1966	Marc Moens	Ghent, Belgium	2:26:45
1967	Jean-Pierre Burny	Brussels, Belgium	2:25:08
1968	Franz Baler	Braunau, Austria	2:18:02
1969	Manfred Pock	Klagenfurt, Austria	2:15:37
1970	Berndt Kast	Ulm, W. Germany	1:58:41
1971	Art Viteralli	Newport Beach, CA	2:07:28
l972	Art Viteralli	Newport Beach, CA	2:12:40
1973	Klaus Nenninger	Munich, W. Germany	2:14:55
1974	Gunter Hammersbech	California	2:18:58
1975	Art Viteralli	Newport Beach, CA	2:17:10
1976	Gary Lacy	Silverthorne, CO	2:07:27
1977	Gary Lacy	Silverthorne, CO	2:39:37
1978	Michael Strobel	Munich, W. Germany	1:58:22

1979	Gary Lacy	Silverthorne, CO	2:07:27
1980	Michael Strobel	Munich, W. Germany	1:54:04
1981	Scott Randolph	Silverthorne, CO	2:22:00
1982	Scott Randolph	Silverthorne, CO	2:22:47
1983	Gary Lacy	Silverthorne, CO	1:52:36
l984	Gary Lacy	Boulder, CO	1:56:19
1985	Andy Corra	Durango, CO	1:55:35
1986	Dave Orlicky	Denver, CO	1:58:05
1987	Gary Lacy	Boulder, CO	2:12:32

NOTE: times depend on the river volume as well as the racers' ability.
Source: Salida *Mountain Mail*

Mile 51.7
Geology
Tenderfoot Hill (S Mountain). The resemblance of Salida's Tenderfoot Hill to a volcanic cone is probably coincidental. But the cone-shaped hill with the big white S is a remnant of late Tertiary volcanic activity. Andesite is the principal rock type here. Compared to rhyolite (another lava rock—miles 31, 31.6 and 41.2), andesite has much less quartz and more minerals containing iron and magnesium giving it a darker color. Much of the material in S Mountain is thought to have been transported in a mudflow resulting from a sudden snow melt caused by intense volcanic heat.
History
A Forty Year Record. Out of all the thousands of Independence Day foot races held during our nation's history, none was more noteworthy than Salida's first Tenderfoot Hill Climb held on July 4, 1913. The race course led from

the center of town, across the river on the F Street Bridge, across the railroad, up the 45-degree face of Tenderfoot Hill and back down. One of the competitors in that first Tenderfoot Hill race was Salida's ace runner and state champion in the mile. He had the graceful-sounding name one would expect of a track star—Delacey Ramsey. At the age of 92, Ramsey recalls the event from his Salida home: "I was working in a dry goods store on the day of the race and I asked the boss if I could get the time off to run. He told me to go ahead. I, Delacey Ramsey, was first, and Marshal Demphey, the policeman's boy, was second. That was the first time they ever ran the Tenderfoot Race and I held that record for forty years." Eventually the Tenderfoot Hill Race was incorporated into the FIBArk festivities, but it wasn't until 1974 that Dennis Vitrarelle of Newport Beach, California broke Ramsey's record of 15:07. By then the course had changed a bit as Ramsey points out: "Our race was four blocks longer and we never had a path. Now there's a path." But the biggest obstacles which the racers in the first Tenderfoot Hill Climb had to deal with were the long chains of Denver and Rio Grande Western box cars parked in the railyard at the mountain's base.

Another notable competitor in the Tenderfoot Hill Race is Roy Hicks of Salida. Hicks placed first in 1978, '79, '80, '81, '83, '84, '85 and '86. His course record of 10:48.1 set in 1980 still stands.

Depot Robbery. To the east side of the river at this location was the old Rio Grande depot and station. Several months after the Denver and Rio Grande built their station, a robber accosted the railroad agent, making off with $600.

This story appeared in the *Rocky Mountain News* on August 10, 1880:

The acting agent of the Denver and Rio Grande railway at South Arkansas had just closed up the office last Saturday night intending to go to supper, when a stranger came up hurriedly and said he was anxious to get a ticket to Boston and wanted to head out on the next train. The agent was loath to disappoint a passenger and was about to stamp it when the pretending purchaser sandbagged him, knocking him down. The villain then ransacked the office and secured $600 in money. There is no clue to the thief. When the agent came to his senses, he was quite alone and in a bad fix physically.

Mile 52
History

Memorial Day Tragedy. An old footbridge used to span the river here. Loaded down with spectators for a special Memorial Day celebration on May 30, 1904, the bridge collapsed, dumping ten or twelve people into the river. An article appearing in the *Pueblo Chieftain* (May 31,1904) told the tragic story:

The Women's Relief Corps was to launch a boat made of flowers to honor those who died at sea. . . . Throngs of people lined the Arkansas, and about thirty persons crowded onto a small footbridge which spanned the river at the end of D Street. . . . As the band on F Street struck up the old familiar hymn "Nearer My God to Thee," the Relief Corps launched the boat of flowers and the people on the bridge surged closer to get a better look.

Without any warning the cable snapped, and to the horror of those watching, the platform dropped. . . and people were hurled into the racing river five or six feet below. Ten or twelve people were dumped into the river, four of those were swept away to their deaths. The Memorial Day services that ill-fated day, intended to honor the dead, claimed their own dead.

Mile 54.2
History

Cleora. To the east of the river, near the present-day stockyard, was the old townsite of Cleora, named for the daughter of William Bales, who ran a stage-stop and boarding house about a mile upstream. The Atchison, Topeka and Santa Fe Railroad, planning to run their line up the Arkansas River from Canon City, bought land here and surveyed the site for a future depot and town. Anticipating the coming of the railroad, about 600 people settled in Cleora in the first few months of 1880.

In April of that year, the Denver and Rio Grande Railroad won a court battle with the Atchison, Topeka and Santa Fe, giving them the right-of-way through the Royal Gorge. They had no intention of developing their competitor's townsite, choosing instead to build their station a mile upstream of Cleora. By October, Cleora was only a memory.

"One year ago, it was a city of importance," said the October 26, 1880 issue of the *Rocky Mountain News*. "Now two or three deserted buildings and the rest of the city had been moved up to South Arkansas. . . . The loss to those who purchased property in Cleora is large as is the ill feeling towards the Denver and Rio Grande for not helping to contrive this as the great commercial center of the Arkansas Valley."

THE UPPER ARKANSAS CANYON:
Mile 54.3 to Mile 74.5

Elevation change: 6950 to 6400 feet above sea level.

Mile 54.3
Biology

The Arkansas Canyon (Grand Canyon of the Arkansas). Like Browns Canyon, the Upper Arkansas Canyon between Salida and Cotopaxi is part of the foothills life zone. However, because of its lower altitude the Upper Arkansas Canyon is slightly warmer and receives a little less precipitation than Browns Canyon. Thus, pygmy forests of pinyon pine and juniper are the dominant ecosystem here. Pinyons and junipers often grow side by side in dry, coarse soil. From Salida to Parkdale, the pinyon-juniper forests are gradually replaced by open areas of shrubs and grasses, making a two-day trip from Salida to Parkdale a good way to observe the transition from the lower foothills to a plains environment.

Mile 54.4
Geology

A Tilted Block of Crust. Between Salida and Coaldale the river passes through older rock first and progressively

Fence lizard, the most common lizard along the Arkansas.

younger rock farther downstream through Howard. This seeming paradox resulted when the Earth's crust was broken and tilted. The uptilted end of this crustal block slants to the west. Today, a small section of Precambrian metamorphic rock at the bottom of the block is exposed immediately after entering the Arkansas Canyon. Farther downriver, note the pronounced angle of the Paleozoic sedimentary layers in the cliff faces, reflecting the dip of the crustal block.

Mile 55.1
Geology

Bear Creek Rapids. The rapids below Bear Creek resulted, at least in part, from the rocky debris washed out of the creek following heavy rains (mile 45).

Mile 55.8
Biology

Bighorn. Bighorn sheep frequently visit the river near the Chaffee-Fremont County line. Both male and female bighorns have horns but only those of the mature male develop a curl (miles 40.6 and 89.4).

Scrub Oak. Soon after entering the Arkansas Canyon, scrubby groves of gambel oak appear on the hillsides. This species generally prefers soil with a high silicon content. A good silicon source in this area might be the Precambrian rock exposed nearby.

Ponderosas. Notice the contrast between the large ponderosas next to the river and the small pinyon pines and junipers on the hillsides. Ponderosas can endure very dry conditions. However, they do require more moisture than the pinyons and junipers, and so at this altitude ponderosas are limited to the shaded hillsides and the thin band of moist soil along the water (mile 23). Douglas firs require still more water than the ponderosas. In the canyons above Buena Vista, Douglas firs were the dominant tree (mile 12.4). But here at the bottom of the Arkansas Canyon, where conditions are dryer, Douglas firs survive on only a few isolated patches of moist soil.

Mile 56.3
Geology

Ancient Oceans. After Bear Creek Rapids the river begins its passage through sedimentary layers which record the rise and fall of ancient seas during the Paleozoic Era between 200 and 500 million years ago—over 100 million years before the modern Rockies were formed. The strata are listed in chapter 1, table 1. Basically, the limestone layers evolved from the bottom muck of a deep sea where myriads of limey shells from microscopic sea animals accumulated to thicknesses of hundreds of feet. As the seas covering what is now Chaffee and Fremont Counties receded, sand was deposited in the shallow water near shore. This eventually became sandstone. Most of the shales probably originated as mud from tidal flats and lagoons. Such vertical changes in the rock layers tell us about the advance and retreat of ancient shorelines.

Softer Rock, Milder Rapids. The relatively soft sedimentary rock in the Upper Arkansas Canyon erodes into less abrupt drop-offs and more gradual gradients than the harder igneous and metamorphic rocks of Browns Canyon, the Lower Arkansas Canyon and the Royal Gorge. This makes for less turbulent whitewater.

Mile 56.8
Geology
Natural Arch. As you approach the narrow wooden footbridge near Wellsville look along the left-hand ridge line for a natural arch formed by the action of frost, wind and rain. Natural bridges, on the other hand, are carved by streams.

Caves and a Fossil Fish. The imposing gray cliff on river right next to U.S. 50 near Wellsville is part of the Leadville Limestone. The ocean responsible for the Leadville Limestone must have covered a vast area as this formation is continuous with other thick sea bottom layers including the famous Redwall Limestone in the Grand Canyon. Limestone, being a base, is quite vulnerable to weathering by acids. When rainwater absorbs carbon dioxide from the atmosphere, a solution of carbonic acid is formed. Although the rainwater's acidity is very weak, it is strong enough to dissolve out large caves like those seen here and on the top of nearby Cave Hill on river right. The Harding sandstone is also found in Cave Hill where it contains the fossilized remains of an ancient fish. At one time this fish was the oldest vertebrate animal known to science.

Mile 57.3
Geology

A Fold in the Rock. When a crustal block is tilted, portions may crumple or even break into joints and faults. Just upstream from the Wellsville Bridge a distinct downfolding is visible in the cliff on river left. Around the bend immediately to the left of the bridge note the joints where the strata have been fractured.

Mile 58
History

Wellsville. At one time, Wellsville was known for its travertine quarries and hot springs. To the north of the river were the English and Wellsville quarries which provided the corridor-facing stone in Denver's City Hall and Court House as well as the exterior stone on the U.S. National

Bank. The hot springs were popular with tourists passing through on Denver and Rio Grande trains.

In 1890, Captain Charles A. Pickett, the proprietor of the hot springs, set up an elaborate placer operation in the Arkansas River near here. According to articles in the *Mountain Mail* (June 11, 1956), Pickett's company, known as the Consolidated Missouri Mining and Manufacturing Company owned 2,000 acres of land in Chaffee County and had the first placer operation on this part of the river.

"Leading out of the Arkansas River, a short distance above the placer ground," the *Mail* said, "was a large ditch ten feet wide and four feet deep, carrying water used in the placer machinery. Two large turbines which operated the entire machinery had a capacity of 6300 cubic feet per minute."

Captain Pickett claimed that his placer operation was producing healthy quantities of gold, but the *Mountain Mail* of December 18, 1890 told a different story: "Captain Pickett has returned from Kansas City where he tried to straighten out the affairs of his company. It seems that Rollins Bingham (Pickett's business manager) absconded with funds and the company went broke."

The story went on to say that Pickett then organized a new company, assuming the role of manager. The *Mail* said he owned a large chunk of farmland in the area, and his primary interest was to irrigate. By enticing investors to back him in his placer operation, he paid for his turbines, which in turn provided the power necessary for irrigating his fields.

The *Mountain Mail* quoted one "old-timer" who put it

this way: "There was a little gold in the river, but it didn't match that which Pickett says he took out. I recall just one miner who had a successful operation at that point in the river. He made enough money for beans and biscuits."

Mile 58.2
Geology

Planter's Plus. The Planter's Plus operation in Wellsville on river left, formerly U.S. Soil, pulverizes the local sedimentary rock for use as a soil conditioner, which, they claim, contains 33 trace minerals important to agriculture. The product is especially rich in gypsum.

Biology

Rabbitbush and Sagebrush. Rabbitbush is one of the Arkansas Valley's most common shrubs and is especially noticeable through this part of the river. Late in the summer it is covered with bright yellow flowers. A low-grade rubber can be manufactured from rabbitbush's latex-like sap. During the early 1920s the Colorado Rubber Production Plant in Buena Vista bought rabbitbush root by the pound but the falling price of rubber forced the company out of business. Rabbitbush is often found in association with sagebrush. In the Arkansas Canyon, sagebrush is generally smaller than rabbitbush and has a blue-gray tint (mile 12.4). The foliage of the rabbitbush is light green. On the other side of the Continental Divide, west of Monarch Pass, sagebrush is more abundant.

Mile 58.9
Biology

Junipers. The fine-looking trees along the calm stretch just up river from the warm springs at Swissvale are junipers. Their full, symmetrical shape contrasts with the gnarled individuals of the same species growing in poorer locations. Juniper wood is often used for fenceposts because insects don't seem to like its flavor.

Kingfishers. This handsome bird is common through this part of the river. Its loud, rattling call is usually the first signal of the kingfisher's presence as it flees in advance of approaching boats. Eventually it will probably fly back upstream to its original spot and this is the time to get a quick look at its striking crest and markings. Also notice its oversized head and bill, designed for nabbing small fish which it pounces on from overhanging branches. Unlike most bird species, the female kingfisher, with her distinctive rusty chest band, is more colorful than the male.

Mile 59.2
Geology

Hot Springs Deposits. The water in the tiny falls on river left was heated by contact with hot rocks deep beneath the earth's surface. Because of its high temperature, the water was able to dissolve and carry in solution a large concentration of minerals. As the water surfaced, it cooled off and the minerals came out of solution, just like the sugar at the bottom of a cooling cup of tea. In this way, the minerals were deposited as the crumbly gray-colored rock surrounding the falls. (NOTE: This is private property—don't trespass.)

Mile 59.7
Geology

The Ancestral Rockies. Between Swissvale and Howard, redbeds of the late Paleozoic Minturn and Sangre de Cristo formations dominate the canyon walls along the river. Many of these sediments washed down from the ancestral Rockies which existed approximately 300 million years ago (table 1)—well over 200 million years before the modern Rockies. The ancestral Rockies in Colorado consisted of two ranges, Uncompahgria and Frontrangia. Both ranges were surrounded by saltwater. Uncompahgria extended across the southwestern corner of the state from the San Luis Valley to the Grand Junction area. Frontrangia paralleled the modern Front Range some 40 miles to the west and was the source of the redbeds seen here. Sediments washing down the other side of Frontrangia are partly responsible for the rock formations in Red Rocks Park near Denver, Garden of the Gods in Colorado Springs, and the Flatirons west of Boulder. All these layers were tilted during the formation of the modern Rockies.

Mile 61.3
Biology

Cactus. Just above Badger Creek, the branching stems and bright red flowers of the cholla cactus first make their appearance. The prickly pear is the other common cactus

Webster Park with cholla cactus in foreground.

along the river. Prickly pears have flat pods with yellow blossoms and are more widely distributed than the cholla.

Mile 61.4
Geology

Lava and Ash. The vertically jointed rock on the hilltop just upstream from Badger Creek on river right is an additional remnant of Tertiary volcanic activity.

Mile 61.8
Geology

Badger Creek Flood. The giant boulder in the middle of Badger Creek Rapid was washed out of Badger Creek by a flash flood in August of 1978. The volume of the creek

during the flood was many times that of the river itself.
Witnesses say the river rose at least eight feet and was
backed up to the Rincon BLM area at mile 61.2. As in any
semiarid environment, flash floods caused by summer
thunderstorms are one of the principal agents of erosion and
deposition in the Arkansas' side canyons. In the summer of
1984, Highway 50 between Salida and Swissvale was
closed twice due to flash-flood damage.

Mile 63.3
Biology
    Willows and Redwings. Willow thickets are the most
common riparian habitat on the thin flood plains lining the
river through the Arkansas Canyon. They are especially
well represented where the river opens up into Pleasant
Valley and farther downstream in Webster Park above
Parkdale (mile 97.5). In spring and early summer, redwing
blackbirds defend their territories among the willows with
calls and displays of their colorful wing patches. During
low water, the willows' roots are visible as a thin red band
at the water line. In winter, the willows' red stems also add
color to the shoreline.

Mile 63.8
Biology
    Barn Swallows. The buildings around Howard provide
good habitat for barn swallows, the only U.S. swallows with
a forked, swallow tail.

Mile 64
Geology

Sangre de Cristo Mountains. At Howard the jagged peaks of the Sangre de Cristos come into view on river right. The Sangres are one of the world's narrowest ranges—only 20 miles in some places. The two pyramid-shaped peaks are the Twin Sisters. Geologists regard the Sangres as a horst—a crustal block elevated between two adjacent lower standing blocks or grabens. The graben to the east of the Sangres is the Wet Mountain Valley (mile 97.5) and that to the west is the San Luis Valley. The San Luis Valley occupies the southern part of the Rio Grande Rift.

Rocks Raised High. Much of the Sangre de Cristo Range is capped with late Paleozoic sedimentary layers. A small portion of slanting Paleozoic sediments is readily visible on the southeast side of Bushnell Peak, the first summit south of the Twin Sisters. This fragment was once continuous with the sedimentary layers seen in the Upper Arkansas Canyon around Wellsville and Swissvale (mile 56.3).

History

Howard. In the spring of 1880, the Denver and Rio Grande built a station near the river at this location. The station and the surrounding settlement were named for John Howard, who settled in 1876 on the nearby creek that also bears his name.

In 1902, the Colorado Fuel and Iron Company (CF&I) discovered a limestone deposit in the hills south and west of Howard. The Denver and Rio Grande built a 5.83-mile-long spur track up a series of switchbacks, gaining almost a thousand feet of elevation between Howard and the mining area which came to be known as Calcite. CF&I built accommodations for 200 miners at Calcite, where they continued to mine limestone until 1929.

Because of a slumping economy, CF&I shut down the quarry that year, removing their equipment and buildings. In 1936, the Rio Grande ripped out the tracks from the old Calcite spur.

Mile 65.3
Biology
Cottonwoods and Woodpeckers. The presence of white, wrought iron fencing notwithstanding, the stretch of river through Howard contains some picturesque riparian habitat. Of special note are the cottonwoods because of their importance to wildlife (mile 44). The center of a cottonwood tree rots out in such a way that it provides homes for many animals. Thus, cottonwoods should never be cut down even if they are dead. Lewis' woodpeckers can sometimes be seen flying between the cottonwoods around Howard. Flickers are the most common woodpecker along the Arkansas.

Mile 65.9
Geology
More Volcanics. Rhyolite, produced by mid-Tertiary volcanic ash flows, occurs on river left from the vicinity of the second Howard Bridge to a point just above Tincup Rapid at mile 67.1. These volcanics can be distinguished from the granitics of the Arkansas Hills to the north by their

redder tone and more jagged appearance. Ash flows consist of hot, ash-like volcanic material suspended in incandescent gas. The particles were probably so hot that they quickly fused together as soon as they stopped moving (see mile 41.2).

Mile 66.3
Geology

Glacial Outwash. The Sangre de Cristo Mountains are high enough to have experienced glaciation during the ice ages. Sediments deposited by streams of glacial melt water flowed down from the Sangres and forced the Arkansas against the southern margin of the Arkansas Hills. At the south end of Howard above Tincup Rapid these deposits are visible as high, stepped terraces on river right.

Mile 66
History

Charcoal Kilns. Charcoal kilns like the large, bee-hive-shaped structures located north of the river near the second Howard bridge were one of the Arkansas Valley's leading industries in the 1880s. Charcoal made from pinyon pines in these kilns was used in the Leadville smelters. In 1889, there were as many as seven kilns near Texas Creek (mile 83.7).

Because of the tremendous heat generated from burning pinyon in these kilns, they occasionally caught on fire. The Salida *Mail* of May 13, 1887 reported that "the whole country was out fighting the flames" when a number of kilns caught on fire in the Browns Canyon area.

Kilns near Howard produced charcoal for smelters in the Upper
Arkansas Valley.
Denver Public Library, Western History Department

Mile   67.3
Geology

   Tilted Redbeds. Just below Tincup Rapid, the redbeds
on river left stand almost straight up and down. They were
shoved into this position by the giant block of Precambrian
granitics which rose on the northeast side of the massive
Pleasant Valley Fault (mile 70.4).

Mile   69.8
Geology

   Angular Unconformity. Immediately above the Vallie
Bridge on river right, the nearly vertical Paleozoic sediments are overlain by a horizontal layer of recently depos-

ited unconsolidated material. Divergences between the angles of older and younger strata such as this are called angular unconformities.

Mile 70.4
Geology

Following the Fault Line. After the Paleozoic redbeds disappear, the river flows to the right of hard, Precambrian granitics directly above the Pleasant Valley fault line. The Pleasant Valley Fault marks the eastern boundary of the crustal block through which the river had been flowing since just past Salida (mile 54.4). This upstream block (capped by the Paleozoic sediments already described) moved beneath the Precambrian granitics of the Arkansas Hills at an approximate angle of 45 degrees. The open area to the south is Pleasant Valley. At mile 73 the river crosses the Pleasant Valley Fault line as it enters a steep walled canyon.

Mile 71.3
Geology

Gypsum. The scarred hillside east of Coaldale at the base of the Sangre de Cristo Mountains is a gypsum quarry. Gypsum is used in various construction materials and to make plaster of paris. The gypsum here is part of the Minturn Formation and was precipitated when sea water evaporated from coastal swamps and lagoons at the foot of the ancestral Rockies.

Mile 73
Geology

   A Puzzling Course. Geologists aren't sure why the Arkansas takes a sharp turn to the northeast across the Pleasant Valley Fault and into the hard granitic rock of the Lower Arkansas Canyon. A southeast course through the Wet Mountain Valley would have offered much less resistance. Perhaps the river's path was already firmly established when movement began along the Pleasant Valley Fault (mile 70.4). Or perhaps at one time it did pass through the Wet Mountain Valley but its flow was "captured" by a stream cutting headward from the east.

Mile 73.1
History

   Cottonwood Rapids. In the early days of Salida's FIBArk Race, Cottonwood Rapids proved to be the biggest challenge for many of the racers, just as it does today. The *Mountain Mail* (June 20, 1953) reported that "the boaters were mighty skilled at handling their craft, but they all got dunked in treacherous Cottonwood Rapids."

   Twelve boats started the race. . . . For the three or four that made it that far, Cottonwood proved to be a bugaboo. Andre Pean and Jacques Musson tipped and lost five minutes in getting their boat back. Ehrman also went over in his kayak, but kept on going.

   In 1954, two French women (the only female contestants in the race) had a close call at Cottonwood, according to a story that appeared in the *Rocky Mountain News* (June 21, 1954):

The spunky French women, Miss Raymonde Paris of Paris and Mrs. Jeanette Pean of Orleans, both skilled boatmen who have won numerous championships in Europe, capsized just after rearing into the Cottonwood Rapids, the most treacherous stretch of whitewater in the river.

Spectators gasped in horror as the two women were dumped out of their two-seated canoe into the roaring turbulence. They disappeared momentarily but bobbed up quickly and started swimming. . . . Several men pulled them ashore and helped them save their boat. The two women insisted on bailing out the canoe and finishing the race, even though they were not eligible to win anything.

THE LOWER ARKANSAS CANYON: Mile 74.5 to Mile 96.8

Elevation change: 6400 to 5760 feet above sea level.

Mile 74.5
Geology

Pegmatite. Just downstream from the Canyon Liquor Store and Campground, a large vertical band of white rock stands out on river left. This is a pegmatite dike. Most pegmatites have the same minerals as granite, but in pegmatite the crystals are enormous—at least a centimeter and sometimes many meters long. Pegmatites form from gaseous magmas flowing into the rock cracks. Because the magmas contain so much gas, their mineral molecules coalesce easily and thus form very large crystals. The Lower Arkansas Canyon and the Royal Gorge both contain an abundance of pink and white pegmatites.

Mile 75.2
Geology
   Red Rock. The massive red cliffs at Cotopaxi may suggest the sandstone of Canyonlands, Utah, but the rock is actually granitic gneiss (mile 35.5). The color is from the mineral feldspar which turns red or brown when subjected to extreme heat.

Mile 75.8
History
   Bernard Creek. Making their way down the Arkansas River, Lieutenant Zebulon Pike and his exploration party camped in this area on December 29, 1806. "Owing to the extreme ruggedness of the road," he wrote, "made but five miles. Saw one of a new species of animals on the mountains, ascended it to kill him but did not succeed." At this point in the expedition, Pike's party, confronted with heavy snows, constructed sleds to carry their gear.

Mile 75.9
History
   Cotopaxi. In 1880, Emmanuel Saltiel, a Portuguese Jew who owned a silver mine in this area, founded the Cotopaxi Town Company. Prior to settling here, Saltiel had been prospecting near a volcano in Peru, which the Quechua Indians referred to as Coto Pasca. Roughly trans-

lated, the name meant "shining pile"—an appropriate name, Saltiel figured, for the community he hoped would spring up around his silver mine.

In an effort to bring more settlers into the Cotopaxi area, Saltiel approached the officials of an organization known as the Hebrew Immigration Aid Society. During the 1880s, Alexander the Third, the Czar of Russia, encouraged anti-semitism in his country. To avoid persecution and violence, thousands of Jews were forced to emigrate. The HIAS was set up in New York to help Jews relocate to the United States.

Promising "rich and productive farmland" for these refugees, Saltiel managed to convince HIAS officials to relocate a group of immigrants to the Cotopaxi area. He then acquired a $10,000 grant from the Baron de Hirsch Foundation to help establish the colony. In May of 1882, 63 hopeful immigrants arrived in Cotopaxi.

Before long it became apparent that Saltiel had promised more than he could deliver. Instead of twenty houses and five barns, the refugees found themselves with twelve small cabins, many of which were without doors and windows. The twelve 160-acre plots of land Saltiel had spoken of were predominantly located on rocky slopes and ridges. Water for these "fertile farmlands" was scarce, the irrigation rights having been acquired by other farmers.

As one of the colonists put it, "It was the poorest place in the world for farming. Poor land, lots of rocks, and no water. The few crops we were able to raise were mostly eaten by cattle belonging to neighboring settlers."

Because of their isolation and their inability to speak

much English, the colonists were unable to voice their protests. Despite the grueling winter of 1882, the refugees found enough work in the area to survive. Some took low-paying jobs in the silver mine (Saltiel's plan from the very start), while others worked for the Denver and Rio Grande Railroad, sawing and stacking logs in Salida.

The following spring, several colonists went to members of Denver's Jewish community for help. Their complaints resulted in an investigation, which in turn led to a revealing article in the *Denver Tribune*. Hearing of the colonists' hardships, HIAS sent them $2,000 in relief funds, and other Denverites sent clothing and medical supplies. The following year, funds were provided to relocate the refugees. Leaving the Cotopaxi "kibbutz" behind, they spread out all over the West to begin again.

Robber's Roost. This was a nickname for Cotopaxi when the main road bypassed the town to the south and outlaws took refuge here. In 1915 a private contracter working from the west and convicts from the Canon City prison working from the east completed U.S. Highway 50 through Cotopaxi.

Mile 77
History

Gold Tom Park. Gold Tom Park, just north of the river, was named for Henry Thomas, a reclusive prospector who built a cabin here in the early 1880s. Thomas worked a placer near his cabin as well as prospecting in the valley's various mining camps. He must have been reasonably successful, because it is said that he usually carried gold dust around in his money belt—a habit that earned him the nickname, Gold Tom.

Because he was quiet and relatively detached from the rest of Cotopaxi's early settlers, there was a great deal of speculation concerning his background and his various mining ventures. And there were those, perhaps out of envy for the treasures he was believed to have had, who came to dislike him.

George Meyers and Charly McCoy, two locals who, for whatever reasons, had developed ill feelings toward Gold Tom, decided to harass the old prospector one day. Thomas was passing by Meyers' house when they sicced a dog on him. Tom warned that if it ever happened again he would shoot the dog. Despite his warnings, McCoy and Meyers took the next opportunity to set the dog on him, forcing the old prospector to use his gun.

Meyers and McCoy then began to threaten Tom, and he told them that if he ever saw them around with their guns on, he would be glad to have it out with them. Several days later, in June of 1884, Gold Tom had that opportunity. Riding into town, he found George Meyers sitting on a bench outside of Hart's Store. He drew his gun first, but his shot ricocheted off the side of the building, and Meyers disappeared into the store. Gold Tom followed him in, and Meyers, realizing he was trapped, quickly opened fire, and shot Tom dead.

Gold Tom was apparently the first and only man ever to die "with his boots on" in Cotopaxi. His body was taken to Canon City, where an inquest was held. The jury decided that Meyers had killed Tom in self-defense.

Later on, Tom's body was buried in an unmarked

grave. Prior to his burial, someone noticed that his ankles bore scars from leg irons, leading to even more speculation about his mysterious past. Some said that he may have been held prisoner during the Civil War; others theorized that he may have been a convict at one time. More than a few men scoured the countryside around Tom's cabin, hoping to find the old prospector's gold, but no one ever claimed to have much luck. Henry Thomas and his gold remain a mystery.

Mile 80
History

Train Robbery. On August 31, 1891, a band of outlaws robbed a Rio Grande passenger train at this location, making off with about $3600 worth of gold, silver and currency. The following day the story of the robbery appeared in the *Denver Times*:

As eastbound express number four was passing through this deep and lonely canyon whose rugged sides almost overhang the railroad. . . the engineer who kept on the alert for falling rocks was startled by the explosion of a torpedo. A few feet ahead two more torpedoes exploded, which was a signal of danger and at once the air brakes were applied.

Then the sight of a red lantern waving across the tracks caught the engineer's eye. . . . No sooner had the train stopped when seven masked men, each heavily armed, swarmed about the train with drawn rifles, and commanded silence of the trainmen and passengers while the robbery was going on.

Messenger Angell at first refused to open the box,

but the second glance at the rifle held in the hands of the leader of the robbers and the accompanying command to be quick in his work opening the safe, caused him to open the doors. . . .

It seemed the money in the express car was all they cared for as the passengers were not molested and the mail bags remained untouched. They did seem to hold a grudge against fireman Auer, for after compelling him to burst open the express car in the face of a storm of bullets, they took his gold watch and chain. . . . It is believed that the robbers crossed the Arkansas River at the ford about a half mile below where the robbery took place.

The indications are strong that the robbery was planned by residents of this valley. . . . This particular section of country has long been noted as the rendezvous of some of the toughest characters in the state. It is also said to be the home of a gang of cattle and horse thieves and general robbers whose desperate characters are well known in Fremont, Custer, Chaffee, and Park Counties.

The Denver and Rio Grande Railroad hired Gunnison County lawman Doc Shores and famous Indian fighter and tracker Tom Horn to investigate the case. Working off a lead from a gunman in La Veta, the two detectives managed to trail the outlaws down into the Texas Panhandle. In the Canadian River country they apprehended two of the suspects—Peg Leg Watson and Bert Curtis—who were then taken to Denver to stand trial.

Several ranchers from the Cotopaxi area, suspected of

helping the outlaws, were also taken to court. While they apparently weren't directly involved with the robbery, it came out during the trial that Tom and Dick McCoy, along with their neighbors John and Frank Price, had apparently been sympathetic toward the outlaws because of previous disputes with the railroad. Some of their cattle had been crippled or killed when they got in the way of Rio Grande locomotives, and the ranchers claimed that the railroad never offered any payment. Railroad officials said that the ranchers drove their cattle onto the tracks and then insisted that their stock was worth more than their market value.

The court never came up with sufficient evidence to convict the ranchers as accessories to the crime, despite their apparent sympathies toward Watson and Curtis. Watson and Curtis, on the other hand, were sentenced to life in prison.

Mile 83.2
Geology
Migmatite. Beginning a half mile above Texas Creek, migmatic gneiss becomes increasingly common. Migmatites or "mixed rocks" consist of granitics, schist and gneiss. Their existence is used as evidence for a theory that granite is sometimes metamorphic rather than igneous. Migmatite may be an intermediate stage in the conversion of sedimentary rocks into granite by heat and pressure but without melting.

Lit-par-lit. Notice the alternating bands of black rock and pink rock in the cliff face on river left. This type of interfingering is called *lit-par-lit* (pronounced lee-par-lee) meaning "bed by bed" in French. It forms when magma is injected into another rock to form a series of closely stacked layers.

Mile 84.8
Geology

Lava Intrusions. Here and there, the Precambrian rock is crossed by dark bands. Some of these are dark metamorphic rocks but some may be old lava conduits flowing into the 39 Mile Volcanic Field to the north (mile 88). The lava hardened into basalt, a heavy rock composed of approximately equal portions of feldspar and minerals containing iron and magnesium. The high percentage of iron and magnesium generally gives basalt a much darker color than rhyolite and granite (miles 31 and 31.6).

Mile 88
Geology

39 Mile Volcanic Field. The 39 Mile Volcanic Field can be seen by looking up the side canyons on river left. The view is especially dramatic at Echo Canyon where it appears as a thick, jagged layer of dark rock capping the hills to the north. The 39 Mile Volcanic Field is an extensive area of Tertiary lava and ash flows emitted from an ancient volcano which is thought to have been the size of Japan's Mount Fuji.

Three Forks Rapid. Rocks and other debris washed out of Echo Canyon are largely responsible for the formation of Three Forks Rapid.

Mile 88.4
Biology

Sandpipers and Mosquitoes. Watch your step if you stop for lunch at the gravel bar on river left above Lose-Your-Lunch Rapid. You may step on a spotted sandpiper nest. The grassy cottonwood grove here is idyllic but the mosquitoes can be bad.

Mile 89
Biology

Lichens. The green and yellow splotches on the rocks are lichens. The digestive enzymes they secrete to dissolve and absorb nutrients from the rock also speed the weathering process (mile 31).

Mile 89.4
Biology

More Bighorn. Bighorn sheep are sometimes seen across the river from the Lone Pine put in (mile 40.6 and 55.8).

Mile 93.3
History

Old Mose the Grizzly Bear. It is said that Old Mose, one of the West's famous grizzly bears, frequently crossed the Arkansas somewhere in the vicinity of Spikebuck Canyon (just north of the river). While his home territory was near Black Mountain (northwest of Canon City), Mose wandered as far west as the Utah state line, as far north as Fairplay, and south into the Sangre de Cristo range. Stockmen estimated that this griz killed as many as 800 head of livestock prior to his death in 1904.

One old-time cowboy said that he'd seen Mose knock down a running horse with one powerful slap to the withers, killing it with a ferocious bite to the neck. C. W. Talbot, an early settler in the South Park country, said he "was a heap more cunning than a fox. . . . I've never heard of but a few hunters that got a shot at him and when they did it was at long range. . . He seemed to know when a man was armed or unarmed and acted accordingly."

"The stockmen in this country were in fear of their lives on account of the big bear," said Talbot. "There were two or three men that had gone to the hills to look for him. They never returned and their bodies were never recovered."

Despite the stories that Old Mose killed four men during his 35-year "reign of terror," only one of these deaths was ever documented. That story, which appeared in the *Fairplay Flume* in the late 1800s, told of Jake Radcliff's unfortunate encounter with the bear. He was out hunting in southern Park County when he came across Old Mose's characteristic three-toed track (he had lost two toes in a trap several years earlier). Hearing the bear's "well-known death snort," Radcliff turned, saw the old griz, and tried to get off a shot.

But before he could, Mose slapped his gun away, and "grabbed him below the knees, breaking the bones as if they were chalk, clawing him in an unmerciful manner. Radcliff lay perfectly still . . . and sure enough, after inspecting his bloody job, Mose made off in his well-known leisurely walk." (His habit of moseying off into the woods earned him the nickname Old Mose).

Apparently Radcliff's big mistake, other than running across the bear in the first place, was yelling for help. Hearing all the commotion, Mose came back "to finish the job, ripping up Radcliff's scalp, biting through his cheek, and throwing him off into the bushes." When help finally came, Mose was long gone, and Radcliff, miraculously enough, was still relatively coherent. He told his terrible tale as they carried him out on a pole stretcher. He died later that night.

A well-known bear hunter by the name of J. W. Anthony finally brought Old Mose down on April 26, 1904. He arrived in Canon City with 30 hunting dogs, claiming that he was ready to hunt the surrounding countryside until he got the bear or the bear got him. One day, up near Black Mountain, he got his chance.

Anthony fired a number of shots, wounding the bear four times, but Mose kept coming. "He faced me at 11 steps distance and came on with his head low," Anthony said. "I fired at his forehead . . . . He sank down slowly to the ground, raised himself partly once or twice and was still except for his breathing which continued for some time. Even after he ceased breathing, he seemed a threatening dangerous bulk."

Old Mose's hide was ten feet four inches long, and he weighed at least 1,200 pounds. His skull was four inches thick, which apparently enabled him to withstand a number of other bullet wounds over his 35-year life span. Shortly after he died, the *Denver Post* did Old Mose justice when they referred to him as "The King of the Grizzlies."

Mile 94.7
Geology
Slickensides. Immediately next to Shark's Tooth Rapid on river right about 30 feet above the road, look for a smooth, flat surface of rock, scraped clean by movement along a fault. This is an excellent example of slickensides (mile 37.8).

THE ROYAL GORGE: Mile 96.8 to Mile 108.2.
Elevation change: 5760 to 5300 feet above sea level.

Mile 97.5
Geology
Webster Park. Just below the BLM take out above Parkdale, the landscape opens up into the north end of Webster Park. Webster Park is a graben—a block of the earth's crust that has dropped along faults between two higher standing blocks (miles 64 and 97.5). The highlands to the west are the Wet Mountains, and to the east is the Royal Gorge Plateau. West of the Wet Mountains is the much larger Wet Mountain Valley graben.

Niobrara Formation. Soon after the Silver Bridge, exposures of the light-colored, blocklike Niobrara Limestone appear at river level. This is the dominant formation in Swallows Canyon between Florence and Pueblo (miles 118.7 and 123).

Biology

Webster Park. The lowlands bordering the river through Webster Park support willows and other riparian species (mile 63.3).

Mile 98

Geology

Parkdale Inlier. In Webster Park the river passes through the Parkdale Inlier where Mesozoic sediments "lie in" amongst and on top of much older Precambrian rock. Ordinarily, Paleozoic sediments like those in the Upper Arkansas Canyon would come between the Precambrian basement complex and the Mesozoic layers (see the geology table in chapter 1). However, this area was once the site of the ancestral Rocky Mountain chain called Frontrangia, and the Paleozoics which stood atop those ancient mountains (as well as the mountains themselves) were removed before the Mesozoics were deposited. The Mesozoic section here was protected from erosion because it is much lower than the surrounding hills. The term "inlier" is relative. The Parkdale Mesozoic layers may also be called an outlier because they "lie out" and away from similar formations on the plains east of Canon City.

Biology

Tamarisks. A number of tamarisks, or salt cedars, grow along the river through Webster Park. Imported from the Mediterranean for shade and erosion control, the tamarisk has spread along the shores of many southwestern rivers like the Green and Colorado at the expense of native vegetation. Tamarisks were first reported on the lower Arkansas around Lamar in 1913. Since then they have taken over much of the shoreline in this area. Fortunately, the cooler climate along the Upper Arkansas has helped keep them in check.

History

Pike's Realization. Zebulon Pike and his men camped in the Currant Creek area near Parkdale on January 4, 1807. He divided his men up into several hunting parties, one to follow the north rim of the Royal Gorge, the other to follow the south rim.

The hunting parties set out, and Pike took several men with him in an ill-fated attempt to penetrate the gorge by following the river. Due to the narrowness of the gorge, they were forced to wade and even swim in several places. Finally, they managed to follow a steep ravine out to the south rim "with the utmost difficulty and danger." There he hooked up with one of the hunting parties and they returned to their camp near what is now Parkdale.

Neither of the hunting parties had found any game, so the young lieutenant decided to take the matter into his own hands. "I then took a double barrelled gun," he wrote, "and left them with the assurance that the first animal I killed, I would return with part for their relief. About ten o'clock I rose to the highest summit of the mountain, when the unbounded space of the prairies again presented themselves to my view."

It was here that Pike realized that he had been following the Arkansas, not the Red River. "From some distant peaks," he wrote, "I immediately recognized it to be the outlet of the Arkansaw, which we had left nearly one month since. This was a great mortification, but at the same time I consoled myself with the knowledge I had acquired concerning the source of the La Platte and Arkansaw Rivers."

Mile 98.7
Geology

Dakota and Morrison Formations. Within view of the Highway 50 Bridge at Parkdale, the Mesozoic sediments of the Parkdale Inlier are exposed in the hills on the left just above river level. The yellow-white rock is the Dakota sandstone which came from the near-shore sands of a Mesozoic sea. The land here is mostly private so stay in your boat. But if you get the chance to examine the Dakota Sandstone along Skyline Drive east of Canon City you may see ripplemarks, mudcracks and the tracks and trails of seashore animals preserved in the rock. The lower and older Mesozoic sediments of red and gray are part of the Morrison Formation which, in other parts of Colorado, has yielded bones from over 70 different species of dinosaurs. Along this part of the Arkansas, the Morrison was formed in a moist climate from limey swamp muds deposited near the shores of the ancient Sundance Sea which once existed to the north.

Mile 98.8
History

Concrete Silos. The concrete silos on river left at

Parkdale were part of a glass-making factory which operated around the time of World War II.

Mile 99
Geology

Royal Gorge. Just past the Highway 50 Bridge at Parkdale the river cuts into harder Precambrian rock at the eastern edge of the Royal Gorge Plateau. The rock in the Gorge consists of mostly granite, schist and gneiss and is in many ways similar to that of the Lower Arkansas Canyon just upriver. However, judging from the Gorge's steeper, sheerer walls, the crustal block from which it was cut must have been pushed up more recently. The greater age of the Lower Arkansas Canyon allowed plenty of time for its walls to erode into a more gentle gradient than that seen in the Gorge.

It's believed that the Arkansas' course was established before the Royal Gorge Plateau arose. Apparently the river continued cutting downward at about the same rate the rock was elevated. Some geologists think the Rocky Mountains may still be experiencing a general uplift. Even today, the Arkansas Valley experiences occasional tremors. During the area's last major earthquake in the 19th century chimneys were toppled.

History

The First Royal Gorge Boat Trips. In the spring of 1873, two young men set out from Parkdale in a small wooden boat, hoping to navigate the rapids of the Royal Gorge. An account of their misadventures appeared in the *Denver Times* on March 30, 1902: "I was a river driver once," said Hank Myers. "It is about thirty years ago that I served my apprenticeship to the trade and I concluded after that one season that I was not big enough to follow the business."

In 1872, the Atchison, Topeka and Santa Fe Railroad was buying railroad ties from woodcutters up in California Gulch. They contracted with a man named C. M. Scribner to float the ties down the Arkansas River. Under Scribner's supervision as many as 75,000 ties were taken downriver to Pueblo.

When Scribner and his men came onto the Royal Gorge, they sent the ties down, hoping that they would turn up at the lower end of the canyon. Hank Myers continues:

The contractors found that they put in far more lumber than showed up at the mouth of the canyon. The next spring they offered one dollar apiece for ties lodged in the canyon which could be delivered to Canon City.

This was big money and it took me and another greenhorn like myself about two minutes to make up our minds that we could make our fortunes and have some fun at the same time. The other fellow, Todd was his name, was as ignorant as I about river driving. Nevertheless, we got ourselves a camp outfit and boat and took them to the head of the canyon.

The way the water rushed into that hole in the rock would have scared out anyone who had sense enough, but with the dauntless bravery born of ignorance, we never hesitated.... We pulled away from the shore and the boat went faster and faster, with Todd at the oars.

I was about to tell him to go easy when with a swish we shot into that hole in the mountain. Whether that boat went sideways or upside down I never could tell and I modestly refrained from asking Todd, for when I next saw him, he was sitting on a rock letting the water drain from his clothes and whiskers. He was so tearing mad that one could get little satisfaction from him anyhow.

By the time we got our senses collected and began to size up the situation, the boat and what of its contents would float must have been near the outlet of the canyon. We were in a pretty bad fix. There was no possibility of getting back up the canyon for the water completely filled the gorge.

It was cold down there and the roar of the water made anything but music to our ears. Our provisions were gone, the only thing being saved from the river a small coil of rope. This turned out to be our salvation. We got together some timber and made a raft, and had enough rope left for a tail to hold it by.

There was nothing we could do except go on down the stream and watch for a place to climb out, and failing that, go clear through. . . . The sun never shone in there and we never knew but the next hundred feet would bring us to a waterfall where our raft would go to pieces and we would be done for. Besides, we were weak with hunger.

It was on the fifth day of our incarceration, and we were about played out and were talking seriously of giving up the job, when we discovered a narrow washout that appeared to reach the top. We started up it thinking it might end as many others did in a sheer wall of rock. As we toiled up and the cut widened, hope gave us new strength, but when we reached the top we were completely exhausted and hungry as we were, threw ourselves down on the ground and slept soundly.

When we awoke somewhat refreshed, we knew the country and found that we had only two miles to walk to a cabin where we could get something to eat. We had traveled ten miles in that canyon and for years after, the roar of a mountain torrent sent cold shivers through me.

In 1949, two Swiss boaters, Robert Ris and Max Romer, the winners of the Salida FIBArk race that year, navigated the Arkansas from Salida to Canon City. However, they were allowed to portage according to the rules of that first FIBArk race (mile 51), so they only ended up running about half of the gorge.

Tyson Dines of Littleton, John Sibley of Philadelphia, and Raymond Zuberi of France were the first boaters to navigate the Gorge successfully, back in June of 1954.

"Hundreds of tourists and sightseers on the world's highest suspension bridge witnessed the dramatic ride through the boulder-strewn passage," said the *Rocky Mountain News* (June 23, 1954). "Manning an eight man life raft, the three swept down the eleven miles from the west entrance. . . to the east entrance near Canon City in slightly under three hours."

They navigated the whole distance except for one point where they had to lower the raft by ropes over a fifteen foot waterfall . . . . Veteran rivermen of Canon

City applauded the feat as remarkable, even though the low water aided the group by slowing the swift currents. "It was not as hard as the Salida boat race," said Zuberi, "but we had to look out for rocks in a lot of places because the water was low."

Mile 99.5
Biology

What Kills Trees? Dead trees, like the large ponderosa pine skeleton encountered on river right soon after entering the Gorge, are frequently seen along the river. In addition to old age, trees may be killed by bark beetles, lightning, rusts, heart and root rots, various other diseases or excessive flooding, drought or snow.

Mile 99.6
History

The Royal Gorge War. The stone ruins, visible along the north side of the river here, are what's left of the forts built by the Denver and Rio Grande crews during the famous Royal Gorge Wars. It all started in the spring of 1878. Leadville was booming, and seeing the great potential for business there, both the Denver and Rio Grande and its arch rival the Atchison, Topeka, and Santa Fe were anxious to lay track toward the headwaters of the Arkansas. As a result, both lines wanted to establish a right-of-way through the Royal Gorge which they believed to be the best route for westward expansion out of Canon City.

In April of 1878, General Louis Palmer directed his Rio Grande work crews to start building towards the Gorge.

Hearing of his intentions, the Santa Fe management decided to try to block the entrance to the canyon. One of their engineers, W.T. Morley, was sent to establish a Santa Fe worksite there. He took a train to Pueblo where he bought a horse and high-tailed it to Canon City. In his rush to beat the Rio Grande crews to the Gorge he literally rode his horse into the ground. From Canon City he had to cover the remaining distance on foot. Arriving at the mouth of the canyon in the early morning hours he was soon joined by workers from the Canon City and San Juan Railroad (a subsidiary of the Santa Fe).

By the time Denver and Rio Grande engineer James DeReemer and his men arrived at the Gorge, the Santa Fe group was blocking the entrance, forcing DeReemer to detour to the north. Making their way upstream, the Rio Grande crew dropped down off the rim and into the canyon where they set up the first of a series of forts.

Having established their territories, both sides brought in reinforcements. Soon, Santa Fe snipers were firing at Rio Grande workmen from the rim. Rio Grande saboteurs, in turn, were rolling huge boulders down into Santa Fe territory, burying tools and equipment. Despite all the harassment, there were no casualties. The real battle was going on in the courts.

On August 24, Judge Moses Hallet of the U.S. Circuit Court in Denver ruled that the Canon City and San Juan (part of the Santa Fe) should have the right of way through the Gorge. General Palmer and the Rio Grande appealed, taking their case to the Supreme Court.

In March of 1879 the Supreme Court ruled in favor of

the Denver and Rio Grande to assume the right-of-way along the river. However, they would have to reimburse the Santa Fe management for all their construction work. (Santa Fe crews had laid out some 23 miles of rail between Canon City and Texas Creek, while the Rio Grande had built only eight miles of track in between their forts.) Setting a fair rate of compensation would require yet another court battle.

During the summer and fall, while the lawyers were at work once again, General Palmer was intent on preventing any new construction. Gangs of Rio Grande toughs managed to run off most of the Santa Fe's employees who were working in Colorado Springs and Labran (a switching yard near what is now Florence).

Responding to Palmer's strong-arm tactics, Santa Fe saboteurs severed the Denver and Rio Grande's telegraph wires. Reinforcements were sent to their stronghold at the mouth of the Gorge where, at one time, their "army" numbered as many as 1,200 men.

Meanwhile, James DeReemer, heading up the Rio Grande's resistance movement in the Gorge, had his men build as many as 11 new forts. Under his leadership, the Rio Grande held their own in the Gorge, much to the dismay of the Santa Fe management. One day, DeReemer managed to chase off a Santa Fe work crew singlehandedly. He noticed the crew working their way up the opposite side of the river. In an effort to head them off, he offered $20 to any of his men who would swim the river. When his men failed to respond, he swam the river himself, making his way up the canyon walls and downstream to a point above the Santa Fe party. There he managed to roll several large boulders down onto their worksite, stifling whatever plans they may have had.

Tensions were mounting. The Santa Fe management was offering a $10,000 reward for DeReemer's assassination. Governor Pitkin, who in the past was content to let the railroads settle their own disputes, was soon concerned enough to take action. He ordered the sheriffs of Pueblo and El Paso counties to keep the peace at all costs.

Violence seemed inevitable. Then in April of 1880, U.S. Circuit Court Judge Miller rendered a decision in which the Denver and Rio Grande would have to pay the Santa Fe $1.4 million for the right-of-way along the Arkansas River. For once the two rival railroads came to an agreement. The Denver and Rio Grande made the necessary payments and the Royal Gorge conflict was resolved once and for all.

Mile 100.5
History

Old Dam and Pipeline. Some evidence of the Canon City Water Department's dam can be seen where the pumphouse appears on river right. The dam was used to store water for a pipeline, the ruins of which can be seen for much of the length of the Gorge. During the 1960s the dam was dynamited because it presented a hazard to boaters.

Mile 101.1
History

Clark's Hole (Mount Rush). The story goes that the big

suckhole next to the large rock at the bottom of Sledgehammer Rapid was named for a kayaker called Clark. His was the last boat in a line of four. When they came to this hole the first in the line became held by its suction, but he was knocked out by the second boat which itself became stuck. The third kayaker was able to bump the second out, but he, in turn, also got stuck. Then came Clark who nudged out the previous boat, but, you guessed it, fell into the same predicament as his three friends. Eventually Clark was able to free himself and continue the trip.

Mile 100.8
Geology
Geology Near Sunshine Rapid. The horizontal black band near the top of the cliff on river left above Sunshine Rapid is lava which has solidified into basalt (mile 84.8). It was probably one of the many feeder conduits for the 39 Mile Volcanic Field to the northwest (mile 88). These bands of old lava are visible throughout the Royal Gorge and the lower canyon. Cutting across the basalt is a pink pegmatite dike like the ones seen upstream in the Lower Arkansas Canyon (mile 74.5) and in other parts of the Gorge.

Mile 102.3
History
The Hanging Bridge. When engineers from the Atchison, Topeka and Santa Fe Railroad were laying out their narrow gauge line through the Royal Gorge, they were faced with numerous obstacles. Even though their route followed the Arkansas, the grade was steep. Sharp curves

were required in order to minimize tunneling and blasting.

They were faced with their greatest challenge near the middle of the gorge, where the river bed took up most of the canyon, leaving hardly any room for the narrow gauge tracks. Blasting out a huge portion of the canyon walls, it seemed, was their only alternative.

Arthur Alonzo Robinson, the railroad's chief engineer, had different ideas. He came up with the design for the famous hanging bridge, visible from the river here. "When finished it will be a curiosity of engineering," said the *Pueblo Chieftain*.

It was indeed. It was unique in that it didn't cross the river. Instead it was hung along V-shaped girders based on either side of the Arkansas. It is 175-feet long, and was built for less than $12,000. The reinforcement wall on the southern end was built later on in the 1920s to take some of the strain off of the girders.

The hanging bridge enabled Robinson and crew to run their line all the way through the Gorge without building a single tunnel—truly a remarkable engineering accomplishment.

Mile 102.4
History

The Incline Railway. The Incline Railroad, visible to the east of the river, was built in an eight-month period, in 1930–31. Some 49 workers, many of whom had been involved with the construction of the nearby suspension bridge, were employed on the project.

Making enough room for the track required some

drilling and blasting near the head of Telephone Gulch. Hoist machinery at the top of the gulch was used to lower the rails down. Workers were suspended from ropes and cables into the canyon walls to support steel I-beams, which were lowered down on flat cars and set in place with a makeshift crane.

The first passengers rode the Incline's rails on June 14, 1931.

World's Highest Suspension Bridge. On June 5, 1929, construction began on the world's highest suspension bridge, which spans the Gorge here. The quarter-mile-long bridge stands 1,055 feet above the water. As many as 80 men were employed on the project, which was completed late in 1929.

The first step was building the concrete abutments on the rim, to support the bridge's steel towers. Then, one-half-inch steel cables were lowered to the bottom of the Gorge from either rim, and spliced together. These "carrying cables" were used for pulling the larger, three-quarter-inch, trolley cables across the canyon. The trolley cables enabled the work crews to pull across the individual wires for the main cables. Each of the main cables was comprised of 2,100 wires which were anchored to steel pins embedded in granite.

Once the main cables were in place, suspender rods were attached to support the steel girders which made up the framework for the bridge's decking. Two separate crews then began working from both rims, laying down the floorboards. Although there were no casualties during construction, one worker recalled that there were a few close calls because of the fierce winds that occasionally blew through the Gorge.

Since the bridge's official opening on December 6, 1929, thousands of sightseers have come to visit the world's highest suspension bridge. Among them have been a handful of daredevils and adventure-seekers: pilots who have flown underneath the bridge, and parachutists who have sailed off into the Gorge. Several years ago, a number of men, attaching themselves to giant bungee cords, leapt off the bridge and bounced around in midair for the benefit of a television film crew from "That's Incredible."

Mile 102.6
History
Wall Slammer Rapid (Lewis' Wall). The less common name for this ominous rapid comes from a kayaker named Lewis who is alleged to have been slammed against the Gorge's sheer right wall five times.

Mile 107
Geology
Tilted Sedimentary Layers. Near its end the Royal Gorge widens as the river cuts through a very narrow area of Paleozoic and Mesozoic sedimentary layers which were tilted almost straight up and down by the rising Royal Gorge Plateau.
History
Where the River Comes Out of the Mountains. For early explorers traveling west along the Arkansas River, the Royal Gorge proved to be a formidable obstacle. On De-

cember 5, 1806, Zebulon Pike got his first look at the Gorge. "Encamped on the main branch of the river near the entrance of the south mountain," he wrote. "In the evening walked up the mountain. Heard fourteen guns at camp during my absence, which alarmed me considerably. Returned as quickly as possible and found the cause of my alarm was their shooting turkeys." Having seen "the mountain," as he referred to the Gorge, Pike decided it was impassable, and led his party north and west into South Park.

In 1820, Major Stephen Long and a party of 19 men set out from Council Bluffs, hoping to find the headwaters of the Platte River. At one point during the expedition, a detachment of men including Edwin James, a botanist who led the first successful ascent of Pike's Peak, camped near the entrance to the Gorge.

"We have noticed that this particular spot is designated in the language of the hunters as 'the place where the Arkansa comes out of the mountains,' and it must be acknowledged that expression is not entirely inapplicable," James wrote. "The river pours with great impetuosity and violence through a deep and narrow fissure in the gneiss rock, which rises abruptly on both sides to such a height as to oppose an impassable barrier to all further progress."

Old Judge City. When the railroad was pushing its way through the Gorge in 1878, a construction camp known as Old Judge City (the chief engineer's favorite tobacco was Old Judge) was located here. Old Judge City was comprised of numerous tents and even had a main street known as Broadway.

Thousands of men worked on the construction of the narrow gauge line between Canon City and Leadville. The work was at times dangerous, and the pay fairly modest. One contractor ran an ad in the Canon City paper offering laborers from $1.50 to $1.75 a day. After taking out $3.50 for room and board, workers on the lower end of the pay scale were making $5.50 for a six-day week. With the onset of the mining boom in Leadville and other mining camps in the Upper Arkansas Valley, and the lure of making big money in the mines, contractors were hard pressed to keep their crews on the job.

The work was demanding. When it was necessary to blast away at the canyon's walls, men were lowered on ropes with steam drills. After drilling numerous holes in the granite, charges of "giant powder" were placed in crevices, and the explosions would often send house-sized rocks crashing down into the river.

One whimsical account of working on the railroad crews appeared in Ernest Seton's book, *Crest of the Continent.* Colonel Nat Babcock of Gunnison told Seton about blasting out the canyon walls:

One day my boss sez to me, "Do you see that there ledge a thousand feet above us, sticking out like a hat brim?"

Sez I, "You bet I do."

"Well," sez he, "that'll smash a train into a grease spot some day if we don't blast it off."

We went up a gulch and clum the mountain and come to the prissipass and got down on all fours and looked straight down 3000 feet. The river down there looked like a lariat a runnin' after a bronco. I began to feel like a kite a sailin' in the air.

Well, there was a crevice from where we wuz, and we sorter slid down into it to within fifty feet of the ledge, and then they let me down on the ledge with a rope and a drill. . . . When the explosion went off it was wuss than forty thousan' fourth of July's. A million coyotes an' tin pans and horns an' gongs ain't a sarcumstance. The hull gorge for ten miles bellered and bellered, and kept on bellerin wuss n' a corral of Texas longhorns.

Despite the dangers inherent in putting the railroad through the Gorge, only one fatal accident took place. On November 25, 1878 James Ward and Thomas Mitchell were killed and John O'Garry and Pat Rooney were badly injured when a batch of giant powder exploded prematurely.

Grape Creek. The abundance of wild grapes in this area gave Grape Creek its name. "Over the walls on either side of the creek, the grapevines, from which the canyon takes its name, climb in wonderfully rich profusion," said one early explorer by the name of Major Pangborn. "In autumn, the leaves become so delicately tinted, and the vines hang thick with their purple fruit. The effect is something to call to mind, but never to describe." Eugene Parsons, in his guidebook to Colorado, said the grapevines along the creek "hung like Arcadian curtains. . . making bowers of the most exquisite character imaginable."

During Colorado's fur-trading era, between 1820 and 1840, mountain men and trappers frequented the Grape

Creek country in search of beaver. For many years Maurice Le Doux's trading post east of Florence was the nearest center of commerce. There, early frontiersmen like Kit Carson gathered with their pelts to trade for supplies.

In the 1850s Carson led a small cavalry made up of both Mexicans and Americans against a troublesome band of Utes who were roaming this country. Carson and his men built a fort near the headwaters of Grape Creek, which served as a supply base. From there they managed to subdue a relatively large band of Ute warriors.

In 1881 the Denver and Rio Grande Railroad built a narrow gauge line up Grape Creek to serve the fledgling towns of Westcliffe and Silver Cliff. Tracks were laid almost as far as Silver Cliff, but maintenance proved costly because of periodic flooding along the creek. In 1889 a powerful flood destroyed a large portion of the narrow gauge line and it was abandoned.

Biology

What's the Buzz? The loud buzzing sounds coming from the shore below the mouth of the Royal Gorge are from male cicadas—large dark insects with long transparent wings.

CANON CITY TO FLORENCE:
Mile 108.2 to Mile ll6.2

Elevation change: 5300 to 5200 feet above sea level.

Mile 109
Geology
The Great Plains. At Canon City, the sedimentary layers become relatively horizontal as the Arkansas enters the Canon City Embayment of the Great Plains of eastern Colorado. Most of the bedrock here originated from the same late Mesozoic sea which deposited the Dakota, Niobrara and Morrison Formations exposed at Parkdale on the west side of the Royal Gorge Plateau (miles 97.5 and 98.7). For about eight miles past Canon City the river flows through its own post-ice age deposits of humus-rich silt and gravel.

Mile 116
Geology
Pierre Shale. In the vicinity of Florence, the river contacts gray, fine-grained rock that was once part of a muddy sea bottom. Today, it's the Pierre Shale. The bones of prehistoric fish and swimming reptiles are sometimes found in this formation as are the coiled shells of ammonites, ancient relatives of squids and octopuses.

SWALLOWS CANYON:
Mile 116.2 to Mile 141
Elevation change: 5200 to 4800 feet above sea level.

Mile 118.7
Geology

Niobrara Limestone. In the vicinity of the Highway 115 Bridge east of Florence the river begins to pass outcrops of the Niobrara Formation—a series of limestone layers interbedded with shale. This light-colored formation has a sturdy block-like appearance (mile 97.5). Unlike the Paleozoic Leadville Limestone seen in the Upper Arkansas Canyon (mile 58.1), the Niobrara is a rich source of fossil clam and ammonite shells. At Portland (named for Portland, England, where Portland Cement was first made) the Niobrara Limestone is quarried and ground up for cement by the large Ideal Cement Plant.

Mile 123
Geology

Swallows Canyon. A short distance downstream from the cement plant in Portland, the Niobrara Formation forms the walls of Swallows Canyon. At the end of the last ice age, the river may have occupied the entire canyon when great quantities of glacial melt water flowed down from the mountains.

History

The Adobe Curve Wreck. It was two o'clock in the morning, March 16, 1906, and a blizzard was roaring down through the Arkansas River Valley. In a depot near the railroad town of Swallow, a 19-year-old dispatcher was slumped over his set, fast asleep. Beside him was an undelivered message for the westbound train to sidetrack. Half an hour later two steam locomotives, headed in opposite directions, smashed together on what was known as Adobe Curve.

"The Adobe wreck will rank as one of the great railroad disasters in the history of railroading," wrote *Rocky Mountain News* correspondent James Young. "In other wrecks the loss of life has been greater, but none was productive of scenes more horrible."

Rescue teams arrived at the sight shortly after the incident, but by then gas tanks were exploding, driving them back from the wreckage. "They were thus compelled to stand by helplessly and see men and women and children disappear, one after another, in the caldron of flames," according to the *News*. Thirty-five passengers were killed, while many others were seriously injured.

Biology

Cottonwood Forests. In the upper parts of the Arkansas, where rugged terrain limits the size of the flood plains, the cottonwoods grow in small patches. In Swallows Canyon they occur in forests. These are plains cottonwoods. Their leaves are broader than those of lanceleaf and narrowleaf cottonwoods seen at higher altitudes upstream (mile 44). Except for the aspen groves in the mountains, wild deciduous forests such as these are rare in most of Colorado and should be preserved. It is hoped that the land owners along this part of the river appreciate this fact.

Swallows and Great Blue Herons. Swallows Canyon gets its name from the cliff swallows which build their spherical nests on the limestone walls (mile 42.5). Dippers, or water ouzels, build similar nests, but they are constructed of plant material and occur singly. Cliff swallows are colonial nesters and use mud as their principal construction material. The large gray and blue birds in Swallows Canyon are great blue herons. The great blue's stilt-like legs, long neck and pointed bill enable them to catch fish in the shallows.

Mile 140
Biology
Drowned Trees. When Pueblo Reservoir was filled, hundreds of cottonwood trees were drowned. Their tops now project above the water's surface at the head of the reservoir.

EPILOGUE

The Arkansas River is at a crossroads. It hasn't yet been spoiled by overuse and development. But the picturesque ranchlands and cottonwood groves could become prime candidates for housing projects as people discover the high quality of life to be had in the Arkansas Valley. Even now there is talk of building a dam at the top of Browns Canyon. Such catastrophes could be averted if the Arkansas received protection under the National Wild and Scenic River Act. For more information on this subject write or call the Colorado Environmental Coalition (appendix 1).

Appendix 1

Useful Addresses and Phone Numbers

EMERGENCY (sheriff, ambulance, search and rescue)
Fremont County 275-1553, Lake County 486-1249, Pueblo
County 911, Chaffee County 539-2596 (southern), 395-2451
(northern)

AROA (Arkansas River Users Protection Association)
Box 1032
Buena Vista, CO 81211
719-395-8949

BLM (Bureau of Land Management)
831 Royal Gorge Boulevard
P.O. Box 1470
Canon City, CO 81212
719-275-0631

CROA (Colorado River Outfitters Association)
P.O. Box 502
Westminster, CO 80030
303-220-8640

Colorado Association of Commerce and Industry
(for travel information)
Suite 308
1390 Logan St.
Denver, CO 80203
303-831-4711

Colorado Division of Parks and Outdoor Recreation
Department of Natural Resources
13787 South Highway 85
Littleton, CO 80125
303-866-3437

Colorado Environmental Coalition
2239 E. Colfax Ave.
Denver, CO 80206-1390
303-393-0466

Colorado Kayak Supply
22495 Highway 285 South
Buena Vista, CO 81211
719-395-2421 or 395-2596

Colorado Trout Unlimited
1557 Ogden St.
Denver, CO 80218
303-837-1908

Colorado Whitewater Photography
P.O. Box 322
Poncha Springs, CO 81242
719-539-2249

District Chief
Geologic Survey
Water Resources Division
U.S. Department of Interior
Denver Federal Center
Lakewood, CO 80225
303-236-5689

FIBArk Boat Races, Inc.
P.O. Box 762
Salida, CO 81201

Western River Guides Association
7600 East Arapahoe
Suite 114
Englewood, CO 80112
303-771-0389

APPENDIX 2

LOCAL ARKANSAS
RIVER OUTFITTERS

The following outfitters have bases in the Arkansas Valley. They can be contacted for guided raft trips. They can also be called for updates on river conditions and access points but courtesy dictates that their 800 numbers should not be used for this purpose.

American Adventure Expeditions Box 25, Poncha Springs, CO 81242. Based at the River's Edge Motel in Johnson Village. 719-395-2409.

Arkansas Adventures Recreation Ranch Box 1359, Canon City, CO 81212. Based on U.S. 50, 27 miles west of Canon City near Texas Creek. 719-269-3700 or 1-800-892-8929.

Arkansas River Tours Box 20281, Denver, CO 80220. Based in Cotopaxi on U.S. 50. 303-333-7831, 719-942-4362 or 1-800-321-4352 (CO only), 1-800-331-7238 (out of state).

Bill Dvorak's Kayaking and Rafting Expeditions 17921 U.S. 285 Nathrop, CO 81236. Based in Nathrop. 719-539-6851 or 1-800-824-3795 (CO only).

Buffalo Joe Box 1526, Buena Vista, CO 81211. Based in Buena Vista on Tabor St. 719-395-8757 or 303-798-1386 (Denver).

Colorado Whitewater Expeditions Box 187, Poncha Springs, CO 81242. Based at 345 W. U.S. 50 in Salida. 719-539-6072.

Echo Canyon River Expeditions Inc. 45000 US 50 West, Canon City, CO 81212. Based on U.S. 50 near the Royal Gorge. 719-275-3154, 632-3684 (Colorado Springs) or 1-800-367-2167 (CO only).

Four Corners Expeditions Box 1032-B85, Buena Vista, CO 81211. Based in Nathrop on U.S. 285. 719-395-6657, 395-8949 or 1-800-332-7238 (CO only), 1-800-262-5542 (out of state).

Independent WhiteWater Box B, Garfield CO 81227. 719-539-4634, 539-4057 or 1-800-332-3668 (CO only), 1-800-525-9390 (out of state).

Lazy J Resort and Rafting Box 85, Coaldale, CO 81222. Based on U.S. 50 in Coaldale. 719-942-4274.

Noah's Ark Whitewater Rafting Box 850, Buena Vista, CO 81211. Based In Jonhson Village on U.S. 285. 719-395-2158.

River Runners Ltd. 11150 U.S. 50, Salida, CO 81201. Based in Nathrop, Salida and the Royal Gorge. 719-539-2144 or 1-800-332-9100 (CO only), 1-800-525-2081 (out of state), 719-275-2156 (Royal Gorge Office).

Rocky Mountain Outdoor Center Star Route Box 323-A, Howard, CO 81233. Based on U.S. 50 in Howard. 719-942-3214.

Royal Gorge Rafting 45045 US 50, Canon City, CO 81212. Based on U.S. 50 near the Royal Gorge. 719-275-5161.

Royal Gorge River Adventures and Expeditions Box 1359, Canon City, Colorado 81212. Based on U.S. 50 near the Royal Gorge. 719-269-3700 or 1-800-892-8929 (Colorado only).

Sierra Outfitters and Guides 44864 U.S. 50 West, Canon City, CO 81212. Based on U.S. 50 near the Royal Gorge. 719-275-0128.

Timberwolf Whitewater Expeditions Box 573, Salida, CO 81201. Based at 1147 E U.S. 50 in Salida. 719-539-7508, 634-7888 (Colorado Springs), 303-425-6564 (Denver).

Timber Rafting Box 403, Winter Park, CO 80482. Based in Swissvale on U.S. 50. 303-670-0177 or 1-800-332-3381.

Whitewater Encounters 1422 S. Chambers Circle, Aurora, CO 80012. Based on U.S. 285 just south of the Hecla Junction turnoff. 303-751-0161 (Denver), 719-539-7478 (Salida).

Whitewater Voyageurs Box 346, Poncha Springs, CO 81242. Based in Poncha Springs at the intersection of U.S. 50 and 285. 719-539-4821 or 1-800-541-3395 (CO only), 1-800-255-2585 (out of state).

Wilderness Aware Box 1550, Buena Vista, CO 81211. Based in Buena Vista on Cedar Streeet. 719-395-2112.

APPENDIX 3

ADDITIONAL READING

The Arkansas by Clyde Brion Davis (New York: Farrar and Rinehart, 1960). A lively account of four centuries of human history along the Arkansas from its headwaters all the way to the Mississippi.

Centennial by James Michener (New York: Random House, 1974). This exciting, fictionalized story of Colorado from its geological beginnings to the present was made into a TV mini-series.

Colorado by Marshal Sprague (New York: W.W. Norton, 1984). An easy reading account of the state's human history from the Louisiana Purchase to modern environmental questions.

Colorado Whitewater by Jim Stohlqwuist (Buena Vista, Colorado: Colorado Kayak Supply, 1982). This guide to the "difficult Rivers and Streams of the Rocky Mountain Region" is geared towards kayakers and contains a wealth of factual info such as gradients, mileages, scenic ratings, etc.

The Crest of the Continent by Ernest Ingersoll (Chicago: R.R. Donnelley and Sons, 1885).

Ecology of Colorado Mountains to Arizona Deserts by Helen Moenke (Denver, Colorado: Denver Museum of Natural History, 1971). Beautiful color photos of the Dioramas at the

Denver Museum of Natural History enhance this short, informative book about biological life zones.

Floater's Guide to Colorado by Doug Wheat (Billings and Helena, Montana: Falcon Press, 1983). A comprehensive work covering not only the rapids but also the history and natural history of Colorado's rivers.

From Grassland to Glacier by Cornelia Fleischer Mutel and John C. Emerick (Boulder, Colorado: Johnson Books, 1984). The plants, animals and ecology of 13 Colorado habitat types are described in this informative and well-illustrated book.

A Guide Book to Colorado by Eugene Parsons (New York: Little, Brown and Co., 1911).

A History of Chaffee County by June Shaputis and Suzanne Kelly (Buena Vista, Colorado: Buena Vista Heritage Society, 1982). This oversize volume covers the history of Chaffee County's important places and notable families in text and numerous, classic photos.

Knocking Around the Rockies by Ernest Ingersoll (New York: Harper and Row, 1883).

"The Old Colorado Midland" by Linwood Moody, in *Railroad Stories* (Frank Munsey Co., August 1936).

Prairie, Peak and Plateau by John and Halka Chronic (Denver, Colorado: Colorado Geological Survey, 1972). An easy-to-understand overview of Colorado's geology.

Roadside Geology of Colorado by Halka Chronic (Missoula, Montana: Mountain Press, l980). You can learn a lot of geology simply by driving in Colorado—if you have a text such as this. The most frequently traveled roads are covered.

Rebel of the Rockies: The Story of the Denver and Rio Grande Western Railroad by Robert G. Athearn (New Haven, Connecticut: Yale University Press, l962). A must for railroad buffs.

Standard First Aid and Personal Safety prepared by the American Red Cross (Garden City, New York: Doubleday, 1981). This is the text used in many first aid classes.

Tourbook of the American Automobile Association—Colorado and Utah. (AAA, 8111 Gatehouse Road, Falls Church, VA 22047). Good information on the major attractions.

Under the Angel of Shavano by George G. Everett and Wendell F. Hutchinson (Denver, Colorado: Golden Bell Press, l963). A lengthy and detailed history of the Salida area.

NOTES

NOTES

NOTES

NOTES

NOTES

NOTES

NOTES

NOTES

NOTES

NOTES

NOTES